WITHIN
LIVING HIS LIKENESS

SUSAN WIGGS

Jesus Within, Living His Likeness
Copyright @ 2025 Susan Wiggs

All rights reserved. No part of this publication may be reproduced or transmitted in any form or by any electronic or mechanical means including photo copying, recording, or any information storage and retrieval system now known or to be invented, without permission in writing from the publisher or the author.

Unless otherwise indicated, all Scripture verses are taken from the Berean Standard Bible, copyright 2021, Used by permission.

Additional Bible Versions used by permission:

Amplified Bible (AMP)
Aramaic Bible in Plain English (ABPE)
Christian Standard Bible (CSB)
English Standard Version (ESV)
Good News Translation (GNT)
International Standard Version (ISV)
King James Version (KJV)
New American Standard (NASB)
New American Standard 1995 (NASB 1995)
New International Version (NIV)
New King James (NKJV)
New Living Translation (NLT)

ISBN: 978-1-966382-49-2

Cover design: Robin Black
Cover photo: Dan Davis

Published by EABooks Publishing, a division of Living Parables of Central Florida, Inc. a 501c3

EABooksPublishing.com

I dedicate this book to
My Lord and Savior

"I have heard of You by the hearing of the ear,
but now my eye sees You."

Also to
My Late Husband, Evan Wiggs
Who Demonstrated the Love and Power of Jesus

With Much Thanks to

Donna Culmer, Editor- and Encourager-in-Chief!

INTRODUCTION

*And we know he lives in us because
the Spirit he gave us lives in us.*
I JOHN 3:24 NLT

*For God knew his people in advance,
and he chose them to become like his Son.*
ROMANS 8:29 NLT

Has a line in a song ever struck you in an unusual way? At a Bible study one evening, we sang a well-known worship song with the line, "His blood flows through my veins." This was not a literal idea of course; even so I was struck by the image of the perfect, life-giving blood of Jesus saturating every area of my being in the way my own blood does. It was a hopeful, even exciting thought. How would my life change if the blood of Jesus replaced my own?

What would be the effect of the lifeblood of Jesus dwelling within you and me? Would our words and actions echo Jesus' words and actions? It may seem impossible or even irreverent to say that someone could live the likeness of Jesus, being like him, but there are hundreds of scriptures from the Bible that confirm that God gives us that ability when we accept Jesus as Lord and Savior.

Jesus was holy, perfect, righteous, full of love, joy, peace, patience, kindness, goodness, and faithfulness (Gal 5:22). You may already be thinking, "Well, that leaves me out! I could never have all those things!" But we will see it is God's plan for us to have those same qualities in our life. Yes, even the perfect, holy, righteous part! How could that be? The "genesis" of this plan is, "Let Us make man in Our image, after Our likeness" (Gen. 1:26). And that is what he did—"When God created man, he made him in the likeness of God" (Gen. 5:1). Being made in the likeness of God has been described as being given the power to be holy. If that were impossible for man, God would never have commanded, "Be holy, because I am holy" (1 Peter 1:16).

We will never be divine like God the Father, the Son, and the Holy Spirit. Together as one, they are all-knowing, all-powerful, and present everywhere. But there are bold, even startling statements made in the Bible about God's plan for those who believe in him. The apostle Peter says, "He has given us His precious and magnificent promises, so that through them you may become partakers of the divine nature" (2 Peter 1:4). John says, "As [Jesus] is, we also are in this world" (1 John 4:17 English Standard Version); and "The glory which You gave Me I have given them, that they may be one just as We are one" (John 17:22 ESV).

The Bible message is that the power of the gospel of Jesus is not dependent on the personal power of a human. It is totally based on the power of an omniscient, omnipotent, and omnipresent God who came to earth fully God and fully man and has allowed his followers to take on many aspects of his being.

We have heard stories of wealthy people who for some reason live as if they are impoverished. In much the same way, Christians can live in poverty of mind and spirit, not knowing or not accepting the riches God has given them. Paul wrote in Ephesians, "This grace was given me: to preach to the Gentiles the unsearchable riches of Christ" (Eph 3:8).

The Bible reveals that Jesus gives us his life when we believe in him as the Son of God, the Messiah. The Scriptures contain glorious truths and promises about God's gift of salvation and his riches that are meant to give his followers all they need for life and godliness (2 Pet. 1:3). God has led me on a treasure hunt for these riches in the Bible. I am excited to share these with you here!

The psalmist said, "My heart overflows with a pleasing theme" (45:1 ESV). Let's look together at the pleasing themes in the Bible and ask God to give us a new vision of who he is and how he has given us all things for living a glory-filled, joyful, and powerful life. He is always inviting us to receive his life and live his likeness.

CONTENTS

Introduction 7

PART 1: LIVING by the WORDS of JESUS 13
1. Divine Inspiration of the Bible 15
2. Evidence the Bible is True 27
3. Jesus and the Scriptures 37
4. Responding to the Word of God 47
5. Wonders of the Word 55
6. Doing and Delighting in the Word 63

PART 2: UNION with JESUS in the BIBLE 71
7. United with Jesus 73
8. Paul: Christ in You and You in Christ 79
9. Identifying with Jesus in Salvation 85
10. Jesus Teaches Something New 97
11. Jesus Teaches on Union with Him 103
12. Union by the Holy Spirit 111
13. The Advantage of the Holy Spirit 117

PART 3: LIVING in UNION with JESUS 133
14. Living as Children of God 135
15. Forming Christ Within 145
16. Living in the Freedom of Jesus 157
17. Walking the Paths of the Lord 167
18. Doing the Works of Jesus 179
19. Living the Eternal Life of Jesus 191

NOTES 201

PART 1

LIVING *by* the WORDS *of* JESUS

Oh, how I love Your law! All day long it is my meditation.
PSALM 119:97

In Him you also trusted, after you heard the word of truth, the gospel of your salvation.
EPHESIANS 1:13 NKJ

It was smaller than most Bibles. It fit just right in the cargo pocket of my husband's hiking pants. It was his constant companion for years and went with him to South America, Africa, and Asia, as well as the dentist's office and mall (waiting for me!). My oldest granddaughter now has this special Bible, worn but well taken care of, and Evan is in the presence of its author. On earth, he loved God and his Word, and brought its message of salvation to many people. He taught that every word was true, every promise sure, and every act of God done in love. He agreed with David who said, "Oh, how I love Your law! All day long it is my meditation."

Why do we love the Word of God? Why is it our meditation all day long? The Holy Spirit speaks through the Bible and helps us discover the depths and riches of the gospel and God's plan for each of us. Every word is inspired, or God-breathed, and teaches we can trust our holy, righteous, and just God. If we use the Bible as a standard against which we weigh our lives, it will reveal what is or is not of God. It is the ultimate judge of our beliefs, our actions, and our thinking. It teaches what is right and wrong and prepares us for every good work (2 Tim. 3:16–17). The Holy Spirit helps us transfer truth and meaning to our life from the Scriptures. We will find verses that say the very words of God are life to those who find them (Hint: Look at Prov. 4:22).

What does the Bible say about living the likeness of Jesus, being more like him? How do we know he wants us to be like him? Does he help us in the process? Can we receive the life of Jesus? Can we think of his presence in our life as if his blood were in our veins? Because we look for answers to these questions in the Bible, it is important to decide if we can trust what it says.

The Bible has the answer to more questions than we could ask in a lifetime. It tells us the nature of each member of the Trinity. What are they like? Why do they say and do what we read in the Bible? The Bible is the place to start when questioning who God, Jesus, and the Holy Spirit are. Understanding and believing the Word of God is our foundation for being more and more like Jesus.

Some may ask if we can believe the Bible is accurate in history and in spiritual truth. Let's look together at the inspiration of Bible authors; evidence that the Bible is true; what Jesus said about the Scriptures; and how we respond to the words of God.

CHAPTER 1

DIVINE INSPIRATION OF THE BIBLE

*"The grass withers, the flower fades,
but the word of our God will stand forever."*
ISAIAH 40:8

The best-selling book of all time is the Christian Bible. It has been said that 2,500 copies are sold every hour, and that number is skyrocketing. Sales in the U.S. were up 22% in the first ten months of October 2024 compared to 2023 sales during the same period, according to the *Wall Street Journal*.

Research conducted by the British and Foreign Bible Society in 2021 suggests that the total number of Bibles that have been printed in the roughly 1,500 years since its contents were standardized probably lies between 5 and 7 billion copies. This is compared to approximately 1.1 billion copies of *Quotations from Chairman Mao Tse-Tung*, second in number of copies sold; and third, the Quran with 800 million copies sold.[1]

Throughout the ages, the Bible is a book that people have risked their lives to obtain, provide, or to simply believe in. God makes it clear that these wonderful words are meant to give life, peace, and joy to those who hear them. The Bible has endured through the ages, bringing the message of God's saving grace to millions of people.

GOD-INSPIRED SCRIPTURES

Christians who believe the Bible is wholly true with no errors do so because they consider God is the author. The Bible says in multiple places and in many ways that the Scriptures were divinely inspired by God. Believing that God inspired the words of each writer of the Bible is the basis for accepting that what it says is truth. Jesus, the Son of God, said he was the way, the truth, and the life; this means his inspired Word is not only true but also the way to find life. In a day when truth is more and more difficult to determine, we can trust the Bible message to be our standard for truth.

Inspiration and Old Testament Writers

Old Testament authors knew they were recording the words of God himself. Moses wrote the Torah between approximately 1445 BC and 1405 BC. He was not physically present at creation, but he recorded that event in the book of Genesis. It had to have been communicated to him by God, who along with Jesus and the Holy Spirit were all there at creation (Gen. 1:2 and John 1:2–3). Abraham, Isaac, and Jacob with his twelve sons, all lived before Moses, who recorded their story as God inspired him. Moses began writing about his own life in Exodus 2, again inspired by God.

The giving of the Ten Commandments to Moses provides a clear picture of God as author. After miraculously escaping from the Egyptian army that pursued them, the Israelites arrived in the desert where the LORD said to Moses, "Come up to Me on the mountain and stay here, so that I may give you the tablets of stone, with the law and commandments I have written for their instruction" (Ex. 24:12). So Moses went up and when God was finished speaking to him on the mountain…

> Moses turned and went down the mountain with the two tablets of the Testimony in his hands. They were inscribed on both sides, front and back. The tablets were the work of

God, and the writing was the writing of God, engraved on the tablets (Ex 32:15-16).

God had literally written the Ten Commandments on the stone tablets with his finger. Moses had a little bit of trouble keeping the tablets in one piece! When he descended from Mount Sinai with them in hand, he was so angry to see the golden calf that the children of Israel had built and were worshiping, that he threw down the tablets and broke them at the foot of the mountain. He took a new set up the mountain again and God rewrote the Ten Commandments (Ex 34:28). Moses eventually wrote all the first five books of the Bible and even the ninetieth psalm.

David also testifies that the Old Testament Scriptures he wrote were inspired by God. In his last words he said, "The Spirit of the LORD speaks by me; his word is on my tongue" (2 Sam. 23:2 ESV). About 1,000 years later, Jesus himself said that David wrote "in the Spirit" (Matt. 22:43). David was able to not only say he knew what the words of the Lord were but described them as tried, refined like silver in a furnace, and purified seven times (Ps 12:6).

Inspiration and New Testament Writers

Jesus himself told his disciples why and how the New Testament would be written, as well as how he would speak to and guide his followers. He said:

> I still have much to tell you, but you cannot yet bear to hear it. However, when the Spirit of truth comes, He will guide you into all truth. For He will not speak on His own, but He will speak what He hears, and He will declare to you what is to come. He will glorify Me by taking from what is Mine and disclosing it to you. Everything that belongs to the Father is Mine. That is why I said that the Spirit will take from what is Mine and disclose it to you (John 16:12–15).

Jesus knew it was impossible for his disciples to remember all that he spoke about during his ministry on earth. As a result, Jesus said the "Spirit of truth," the Holy Spirit, would come. He, like Jesus, would not speak on his own authority, but would glorify Jesus as Jesus glorifies the Father. This provides a basis for believing in the divine inspiration of the New Testament, which records the birth and ministry of Jesus, the Son of God.

The authors of the New Testament write about divine inspiration of the Bible through the Holy Spirit. This is what Peter, an "inner circle" disciple of Jesus, wrote:

> We have the prophetic word more fully confirmed….
> Knowing this first of all, that no prophecy of Scripture comes from someone's own interpretation.
> For no prophecy was ever produced by the will of man, but men spoke from God as they were carried along by the Holy Spirit (2 Peter 1:19–21 ESV).

In this same passage, Peter uses beautiful poetic imagery comparing the prophetic word to a lamp shining light in the dark place of the world before the morning star, Jesus, arises in our hearts. Peter is emphatic that prophecy of Scripture was not written with the authority of the author, but by the Holy Spirit, who moved men to write what God spoke. While using the writing style and vocabulary of the individual author, the Holy Spirit guided each one to write the meaning of what God spoke, with no mistakes and nothing left out!

Regarding inspiration of the New Testament, Paul, who wrote thirteen of its books, said, "For I would have you know, brothers, that the gospel that was preached by me is not man's gospel. For I did not receive it from any man, nor was I taught it, but I received it through a revelation of Jesus Christ" (Gal. 1:11–12 ESV). Peter said that the wisdom that Paul wrote was "according to the wisdom given him" (2 Peter 3:15). Paul wrote this in his second letter to Timothy, which turned out to be the last he ever wrote:

> All Scripture is God-breathed [inspired by God] and is useful for instruction, for conviction, for correction, and for training in righteousness, so that the man of God may be complete [ready-because-prepared, Strong's 739], fully equipped for every good work (2 Tim. 3:16–17).

Because most of the New Testament had been written by the time Paul wrote this, we can assume that when he said "all Scripture" he meant not only the Old Testament but also what he knew of the New. He was speaking as a seasoned author himself, reporting by inspiration, observation, and experience that God had "breathed" the Scriptures for the writers. What a beautiful way to express that the life of God energizes the words of our Bible!

PERFECT WORD OF GOD

God made sure that his Word would accurately endure through the ages. In his Sermon on the Mount, Jesus said, "For I tell you truly, until heaven and earth pass away, not a single jot [smallest letter, NASB], not a stroke of a pen, will disappear from the Law until everything is accomplished" (Matt. 5:18). It is interesting that Jesus refers to the smallest Hebrew letter, *yud* י. On first look, we might think Jesus is referring to a small, unimportant letter. This is not the case. There is a fascinating study of this letter in L. Grant Luton's book, *In His Own Words: Messianic Insights into the Hebrew Alphabet*.

As he points out, Hebrew letters have great depth of meaning. On their own, each letters represents sounds as well as objects and numbers, but in addition, there is meaning in their shape, size, and position in a word, phrase, or even complete text. The *yud* looks similar to a comma but is "suspended in space," not anchored at the bottom of a word like English letters. Because of this elevated position, *yud* is said to be anchored in heaven, associated with spiritual things, and is even a representation of the Holy Spirit, the very life and presence of God in the believer.

Now you can begin to see the importance of this letter to Jesus and his attention to it as representing the care needed in preserving the smallest written parts of the law that Moses wrote. This attention can even be interpreted as God's concern for what seems insignificant on the surface in life. Indeed, leaving out this *yud* has a powerful effect on word meaning. When *yud* is added to the Hebrew word *shameim* (desolation), it becomes *shamaim* (heaven). No wonder Jesus makes the point that the *yud*, the "smallest letter" and yet critical, will not be left out of the law "until heaven and earth pass away."[2]

PERMANENT WORD OF GOD

In Isaiah, God makes a covenant promise concerning both his Spirit and his words, making them equally important. He says,

> "As for Me, this is My covenant with them," says the LORD. "My Spirit will not depart from you, and My words that I have put in your mouth will not depart from your mouth or from the mouths of your children and grandchildren, from now on and forevermore," says the LORD (Is. 59:21).

God declares that the Bible will stand forever. It is his Word, perfect and permanent, and he gives us his Spirit to help us live with his words continually on our lips and in our heart. About 700 years later, Jesus taught the same truth: "Heaven and earth will pass away, but my words will never pass away" (Matt. 24:35).

TABLETS OF THE HEART

God wrote his commandments on Moses' stone tablets. We read about another kind of tablet in the book of Proverbs, which was written by King Solomon. This concerns our own heart:

> My son, keep my words
> and treasure my commandments within you.
> Keep my commandments and live;
> guard my teachings as the apple of your eye.
> Tie them to your fingers;
> write them on the tablet of your heart (Prov. 7:1–3).

It is God whom we either do or don't allow to write on our heart. The best way to let him write his teachings and commandments on our heart is to read, meditate and act on his inspired Word, the Bible, aided by his Holy Spirit. God's presence and his commandments and teachings were so glorious that Moses' face shone after speaking to him on Mount Sinai. I want that kind of glory written on my heart, don't you? Here is what happened to make that possible for us all!

> For God, who said, "Let light shine out of darkness," made His light shine in our hearts to give us the light of the knowledge of the glory of God in the face of Jesus Christ" (2 Cor. 4:6).

Do you begin to see how God helps us live his likeness? He shined his light in our hearts, revealing his glory to us by sending Jesus the Messiah. How important it is to see the face of Christ through reading the Scriptures! The knowledge and understanding of Jesus that we gain there is light and life to our heart. We're not on our own here! Jesus told his disciples that God would send the Holy Spirit to "teach you all things and bring to your remembrance all that I have said to you" (John 14:26).

Here's a critical commandment God writes on our heart: "And this is His commandment: that we should believe in the name of His Son, Jesus Christ, and we should love one another just as He commanded us" (1 John 3:23). You see, when we believe, then we have the ability to love one another as Jesus loved.

MIRACLE OF THE BIBLE

We pointed out earlier that Isaiah and Matthew, many years apart, wrote the same truth: God's Word will stand forever. The history of biblical writings being gathered together as a cohesive text of consistent themes is witness that the very existence of the Bible as we know it today is nothing short of miraculous. The magnitude of coordination of authors, languages, and places is unique to the Bible. The sixty-six books in our Bibles today were written by forty authors over approximately 1,600 years, in three different languages set over three different continents.

The Bible contains personal testimonies of proven men throughout the centuries. Old Testament characters exhibit the same strong faith in God and his commandments that is found in the followers of Jesus in the New Testament. Each had their own experiences with God and their witness to his nature and power is completely consistent throughout the ages. All these writers of the Bible were flawed men, whose lives were changed and redeemed by their faith in God.

Let's look at what Old Testament writers Moses and David said about the nature of God and the creation story. Then we'll compare what later writers, Paul and John wrote about God and creation in the New Testament. Do you think they will be consistent?

Moses

Nature of God:

For I will proclaim the name of the LORD. Ascribe greatness to our God! He is the Rock, His work is perfect; all

His ways are just. A God of faithfulness without injustice, righteous and upright is He (Deut. 32:3–4).

Creator God:
In the beginning God created the heavens and the earth (Gen. 1:1).

David

Nature of God:
For the word of the LORD is upright,
and all his work is done in faithfulness. He loves righteousness and justice;
the earth is full of the steadfast love of the LORD (Ps. 33:4–5 ESV).

Creator God:
By the word of the LORD the heavens were made,
and by the breath of his mouth all their host.
He gathers the waters of the sea as a heap;
he puts the deeps in storehouses.
Let all the earth fear the LORD;
let all the inhabitants of the world stand in awe of him!
For he spoke, and it came to be;
he commanded, and it stood firm (Ps 33:6–9 ESV)

Paul

Nature of God:
For the kingdom of God is not a matter of eating and drinking but of righteousness, peace and joy in the Holy Spirit.
For whoever serves Christ in this way is pleasing to God and approved by men (Rom. 14:17–18).

Creator God:
For what may be known about God is plain to them because God has made it plain to them. For since the creation of the world God's invisible qualities, His eternal power and divine nature, have been clearly seen, being understood from His workmanship, so that men are without excuse (Rom. 1:19–20).

Apostle John
Nature of God:
"For God so loved the world, that he gave his only Son, that whoever believes in him should not perish but have eternal life" (John 3:16, words of Jesus, ESV).

Creator God:
Through Him all things were made, and without Him nothing was made that has been made (John 1:3).

Over a period of 1,600 years that the different Bible authors wrote, their reports of God's nature and his creation story are amazingly consistent. The logical conclusion is that each author quoted above, Moses, David, Paul, and John, was divinely inspired by our God who is the same yesterday, today, and forever. These authors are only four of the forty writers of our Bible, but it is certain that the themes of creation and of a righteous, loving God and his plan for reconciliation of man to himself remains the same throughout the Bible. Ultimately, God is the author of the Bible.

Contemplating His Ways:

Why do you believe the Bible is true?

What passage from the Bible has brought you joy, peace, or comfort in the last few days? Was that the Holy Spirit speaking to you?

How could having the Word of God in your heart and in your mouth be a part of living the likeness of Jesus?

What words did Old Testament and New Testament writers use to describe the nature of God? What word or idea means the most to you right now? What might God be saying to you in that choice?

CHAPTER 2

EVIDENCE THE BIBLE IS TRUE

Test all things. Hold fast to the good.
1 THESSALONIANS 5:21

To believe that there is only one true God who is the inspiration behind the Bible is largely a matter of faith, but archeological, statistical, and geographical facts also support the truth of the Bible.

ARCHEOLOGICAL EVIDENCE

In 1947, a shepherd boy threw a rock into a cave high up on the side of a barren, rock mountain in the desert area near the Dead Sea. He heard a sound like ceramic breaking. He discovered what has turned out to be the greatest archeological find of the twentieth century, the Dead Sea Scrolls. Over the next nine years, parts from each book of the Old Testament, except for Esther, were found across eleven caves in the Dead Sea area. At the Qumran archeological site in the West Bank, I got to see the small dark entrance of several of the numbered caves high up on the steep golden stone mountains where the scrolls were found. By 2021, more than 500 caves in the area had been excavated in search of any remaining scroll fragments.

The Dead Sea Scrolls are more ancient than any other known biblical text. Before their discovery, the oldest complete Hebrew texts were the

Aleppo Codex and the Leningrad Codex, both dated to the 10th century AD. The earliest Dead Sea Scrolls are now dated using AI, from the 300s BC, much earlier than previously thought.[3]

The number of scrolls containing copies of individual books of the Old Testament gives an indication of each book's importance to the Jewish community at that time. Psalms, Deuteronomy, Genesis, and Isaiah were the most common and probably most important.[4] It is interesting that these four books are also often quoted in the New Testament, Jesus quoting from Deuteronomy more than any other book. You may agree along with me and the Dead Sea Scroll writers, that the book of Psalms, copied 42 times, is our favorite!

Speaking of Psalms, an exciting discovery was made about the 13th verse of Psalm 145. Before the Dead Sea Scroll copy was discovered, the verse read:

"Your kingdom is an everlasting kingdom, and Your dominion endures through all generations."

A last sentence was discovered in the scrolls, and newer Bible translations now read:

> Your kingdom is an everlasting kingdom, and Your dominion endures through all generations. The LORD is faithful in all His words and kind in all His actions.

I love this verse, incomplete for thousands of years and yet with the same message as every other book of the Bible! It speaks of a powerful God reigning forever as King, but at the same time faithful and kind toward us. It was not present in the 10th Century texts of the Bible, which were the basis for our modern-day translations but has been added to most Bible translations that were completed after the Dead Sea Scroll discoveries. Psalm 145 is an acrostic poem from which one of the Hebrew letters was missing in the Masoretic Text. The missing letter and sentence, "The LORD is faithful in all His words and kind in all His actions," truly demonstrates God's faithfulness by preserving these missing words. Can you imagine the excitement felt by the translators who discovered this text, hidden for thousands of years! Finding the Dead Sea Scrolls proves what the verse says is true: "[God's] kingdom is an everlasting kingdom….and [He] is faithful in all His words."[5]

There is 95% accuracy between the texts that were used for our modern Bible translations and the Dead Sea Scroll texts. Small changes in lettering and a few textual changes such as the Psalm 145 discovery do not change meaning or contradict other writing. The Dead Sea Scrolls have given us confidence that our Old Testament manuscripts are reliable, and that God has preserved his Word through the centuries, kept it alive, and guarded it against error.

Another important archeological discovery of a different type was made in 1993. In the early 1980s, scholars were making the charge that the Bible was just a mythological story. They said historical evidence was needed, not just the Bible, to prove Bible characters and places actually existed. The discovery of the Tel Dan Stela provided that kind of proof. This stone marker, discovered in Dan, northern Israel, written in Aramaic, said, "I killed seventy kings. . . . I killed Joram . . . king of Israel, and I killed Ahaziahu . . . of the House of David." This inscription was a stunning find because it was the first time the name of David was found outside of the Bible and confirmed that he was head of a kingly dynasty. The stela was most likely a monument made by Hazael, king of Aram-Damascus, commemorating his victory over these kings. This stela is important also because it validates the biblical account of Hazael and his victory over Ramoth-Gilead around 841 BC as recorded in 1 Kings 19 and 2 Kings 8–13.[6]

The archeological finds we have looked at and the many that are discovered every year in Israel are pieces of a puzzle that give the world a clearer picture of the land promised to the children of Israel, the biblical record, and the God of the Bible.

FULFILLED PROPHECY AND GEOGRAPHY

The land of Israel itself is fulfilling the prophecies of Isaiah in the Bible. The following Bible verses were inspiration for David Ben-Gurion

(1886–1973), known as the father of modern Israel, and the first prime minister. He spent his last years living in the Negev Desert and famously said that Israel's future lies in the Negev. A statue of Moses, who led the children of Israel in the desert for forty years, rests on a shelf across from his desk, in his home now open to visitors. On that desk are verses he copied and displayed from Isaiah who prophesied in ancient times about the desert land:

> The wilderness and the land shall be glad; the desert will rejoice and blossom like a rose; it will bloom profusely and rejoice with joy and singing (Is. 35:1–2a).
>
> Behold, I am about to do something new; even now it is coming. Do you not see it? Indeed, I will make a way in the wilderness and streams in the desert (Is. 43:19).
>
> For the LORD comforts Zion; he comforts all her waste places and makes her wilderness like Eden, her desert like the garden of the LORD; joy and gladness will be found in her, thanksgiving and the voice of song (Is. 51:3 ESV).

Ben-Gurion was convinced that the Negev Desert would someday blossom and rejoice as Isaiah prophesied. This desert that covers 60 percent of the land of Israel is home to about 10 percent of the population. Today it is indeed blossoming with huge agricultural communities using new innovative technologies to make use of the desert land, so that Israel is able to export half of its produce. Scientists at the Ben Gurion University of the Negev have successfully found ways to use the mile deep aquifers for watering plants, despite the high salt content of the water. In addition to water study, the university focuses on food production and energy production. Today Israel leads the world in desert agriculture, sharing technologies with other countries. It is the only country where the desert is shrinking instead of expanding, demonstrating the truth of what Zephaniah wrote: "I will give you fame and praise among all the peoples of the earth." (3:20).[7]

Israel is the most technologically sophisticated country in the world per capita according to Victor David Hanson. They share much of their agricultural, medical, military, and rescue innovations with the United States as well as with other countries. This is the fulfillment of God's covenant with Abraham, the father of the nation of Israel, in Genesis 2, "I will make you into a great nation, and I will bless you; I will make your name great, so that you will be a blessing" (v. 2). This world standing is even more impressive because the Jews were driven from their homeland and were dispersed among many nations, but miraculously returned and became a nation "in a day", May 14, 1948 (See Is. 66:8 and Jer. 30:18–22). Today, Forbes lists Israel, a country the size of New Jersey, in the top ten most powerful countries in the world.

FULFILLED PROPHECY AND STATISTICS

One definition of prophecy is the declaration of future events such as no human wisdom or forecast is sufficient to make. Bible prophecy is understood to be from God. The one to deliver the prophecy would be considered a prophet of God, or someone used by God to deliver his message with specific, detailed events that might occur years or sometimes centuries in the future. Over 25 percent of the Bible is prophecy so there are many opportunities to see if the prophecies have or have not come to pass. Moses made it clear that if a prophecy spoken in the name of the Lord does not happen, that prophecy was not spoken by the Lord (Deut. 18:22).

I'm not a "mathemagician" so I will refer to Hugh Ross, a well-known Christian astrophysicist who was a skeptic until he became convinced by evidence that the Bible is true. He made this astounding statement: "Stating it simply, based on [the chance probability of] thirteen prophecies alone, the Bible record may be said to be vastly more reliable than the second law of thermodynamics." I knew this had to be a big deal, and it is. That law of thermodynamics says that heat will never flow from a cold body to a hot body. In other words, pouring cold water into a cup of coffee will not make the coffee hotter. Ross bases his comparison on only thirteen Bible prophecies that have been fulfilled even though he estimates there are approximately 2,500 prophecies in the pages of the Bible, and about 2,000 have already been fulfilled to the letter with no errors. He singles out thirteen and computes the statistical probability of each one occurring by chance alone. We won't look at all thirteen, but here are three examples of prophecies concerning the coming of Jesus as Messiah along with his computed probability.

> Prophecy: Prophet Micah (5:2) in 700 BC named the tiny village of Bethlehem as the birthplace of Israel's Messiah. This is a widely accepted fact of history.
>
> *(Probability of chance fulfillment: 1 in 10^5)*
>
> Prophecy: Prophet Zechariah (11:12–13) in the fifth century BC declared that the Messiah would be betrayed for the price of a slave—thirty pieces of silver, which would be used to buy a burial ground for poor foreigners. Bible writers and secular historians both record that Judas Iscariot was paid thirty pieces of silver for betraying Jesus, and the money was used to buy burial land for the poor (Matt. 27:3–10).
>
> *(Probability of chance fulfillment = 1 in 10^{11})*
>
> Prophecy: About 400 years before crucifixion was used, Israel's King David (Ps. 22 and 34:20) and the prophet Zechariah (12:10) described the Messiah's death in words that perfectly fit that manner of execution. They said the body would be pierced but none of the bones would be broken, contrary to custom for crucifixion. Historians and New Testament writers confirm the fulfillment. None of Jesus' bones were broken due to his swift death. His side was pierced with a spear to verify his death.
>
> *(Probability of chance fulfillment = 1 in 10^{13})*

Adding the exponents of all thirteen probability figures (we listed only three here), Ross estimates the odds for all these prophecies being fulfilled by chance without error is about one in 10^{138}! This brings us back to the second law of thermodynamics. For sake of comparison, Ross calculates the chances that heat will flow from a cold body to a hot body = 1 in 10^{80}. He concludes, "Stating it simply, based on these thirteen prophecies alone, the Bible record may be said to be vastly more reliable than the second law of thermodynamics."[8]

Ross estimates that at least 500 Bible prophecies about the "time of the end" remain unfulfilled. He asks, given that the Bible proves to be so reliable, and there is every reason to believe that the end time prophecies will be fulfilled, how can anyone ignore these coming events? Would a reasonable person take lightly God's warning of judgment for those who reject the truth about Jesus, and his offer of salvation?

CHANGED, DEVOTED LIVES

Jeremiah was a devoted prophet, faithful to proclaim the true Word of God even when it put him in great hardship and peril. He was just one of the many Bible characters who risked their lives or were killed for their belief in the God of the Bible. Would they have laid down their lives if they had not been totally convinced of God's truth?

Jeremiah's Rescue
Chaldeans from Babylon were besieging Jerusalem in the time of Jeremiah, but when the Egyptians came to help Jerusalem, they retreated. At this time, God spoke to Jeremiah, "Tell the king, 'Listen, Pharaoh's army that came up to help you will return to Egypt, and the Chaldeans will come back and take this city and burn it with fire. Don't try to say they won't come back because they will, and they will burn the city.'" The princes were so mad at Jeremiah for saying this that they beat him and put him in a dungeon. After many days, the king called for him. "Is there any word

from the Lord?" he asked. Jeremiah, faithful to tell what God revealed to him, said, "Yes, the king of Babylon will defeat you and take you captive."

The princes, Gedaliah and Jucal, among others, heard that Jeremiah was prophesying to the people, "If you remain in Jerusalem, you will die by the sword, or famine, or pestilence. But if you surrender to the Chaldeans, you will live." The princes reported to the king that Jeremiah was weakening the army and the people with these words, and should be put to death. They took Jeremiah and lowered him with ropes into a pit with only mud at the bottom, leaving him to die.

When Ebed-Melech the Ethiopian, one of the king's eunuchs, heard that they had put Jeremiah in the pit, he went to the king and said, "My lord the king, these evil men have thrown Jeremiah the prophet into a pit, and he will die."

Then the king commanded Ebed-Melech to save Jeremiah from this cruel death. In a touching detail of this story, the eunuch demonstrated his tender, compassionate heart; he took old clothes and rags to the pit and told Jeremiah, "Please put these old clothes and rags under your armpits, under the ropes." So, they rescued Jeremiah, but he remained in the court of the prison.

The rest of the story is that God later used Jeremiah to speak to Ebed-Melech and say, "I will deliver you in the day that the city falls. You will not fall by the sword, but your life will be saved because you have put your trust in Me." We can be certain that God's word to Ebed-Melech was fulfilled just as he said (taken from Jer. 37–39).

Another "rest of the story" is that the personal seals (bullae) bearing the names of Gedaliah and Jucal (Jer. 38:1), enemies of Jeremiah, were found in the City of David excavations in Jerusalem in 2005. In addition, the destruction layer of ash from the 586 BC burning of Jerusalem by the Babylonians is clearly seen in those excavations. These discoveries are important for proving the authenticity of the Bible.

The devotion to God in countless people over thousands of years, from fishermen who abandoned boats and nets to follow Jesus, to those who abandon sinful lifestyles to follow him today, prove the power and truth of the God of the Bible. Many believers through the ages lost their lives because of their faith in Jesus, the way, the truth, and the life. Even before Jesus came to earth, Old Testament heroes of faith in God, "*people of whom the world was not worthy*," were tortured, stoned, sawn in two, and put to death with the sword (See Heb. 11:37–38).

This complete faith is again illustrated at the time when many of Jesus' disciples other than the twelve, left him when they were offended by what Jesus taught. When he asked the twelve if they also wanted to go away, Peter said, "Lord, to whom shall we go? You have the words of eternal life, and we have believed, and have come to know, that you are the Holy One of God" (John 6:68–69). When Jesus sent out his twelve disciples, he gave them specific instructions and prepared them for rejection and even death. He told them, "Do not be afraid of those who kill the body but cannot kill the soul. Instead, fear the One who can destroy both soul and body in hell" (Matt. 10:28). Most of those twelve were in fact killed, but they all believed Jesus when he said their body might die, but their soul would not.

We who are persuaded of the truth of the Bible and embrace it, have this great promise of Jesus for today: "Because you have seen Me, you have believed; blessed are those who have not seen and yet have believed" (John 20:29).

Contemplating His Ways:

High tech startups are a large part of Israel's economy. Do a little research in some of those technologies, such as water desalination, agriculture, medicine, and defense. How is Israel fulfilling the Genesis 21:18 prophecy, "And through your [Abraham's] offspring all nations of the earth will be blessed, because you have obeyed My voice"?

Have you or someone you know been persecuted for their faith in God? Did it help or hurt their faith?

Peter said, "We have come to know" you are the Messiah. It was a process of following Jesus, watching him and listening to him that led his disciples to believe in him. Where are you in that process? How can you follow and listen to Jesus today?

CHAPTER 3

JESUS AND THE SCRIPTURES

"If you love me, you will keep my commandments."—Jesus
JOHN 14:15

When I was twelve, like every other year when I was growing up, I went with my family to church every Sunday morning, Sunday night, and Wednesday night for prayer meeting. It was a very special time if we stopped at the local drugstore after church on Wednesday. Stores were closed on Sunday, so even though this is a distant memory, it had to be Wednesday! My dad would get out of the car, go in, and come out with six candy bars. They were a nickel each, but if you got six, you got them for a quarter! We were a family of five, so guess who got two candy bars! (It wasn't me or my sisters or mother!) The faithfulness that we practiced in going to the house of God and worshiping with our fellow Christians was one of the most important lessons of my childhood and lay the foundation for my adult life. It was there I experienced my first conscious thought of Jesus as my Savior and Lord. Our devoted Sunday school teachers taught us all the Bible stories and how to accept Jesus as Savior. As far as I know, I was never left behind when my parents headed for home.

But Jesus was! When he was twelve, he made what was likely his first trip up to Jerusalem from Nazareth for the Passover Feast. As Alfred

Edersheim writes, upon entering Jerusalem, Jesus' "one all-engrossing thought would be of the Temple." As grand as the building was, the temple was even more glorious for the young Jesus as a place to listen to the Sanhedrin teachers and ask them questions. This absorption in the teaching there may have called out his first conscious thought that the grand temple was the house of his Father, and with that also the first conscious thought of his own mission and being.[9]

All the teachers in the temple were astonished at his understanding of their teaching of the Scriptures and his answers to questions. He was so absorbed there that he didn't think about his parents who were frantically looking for him when they realized after a day, that he wasn't traveling home with their company. It is then that we learn the first recorded words of Jesus, "Why were you looking for Me? . . . Did you not know that I had to be in My Father's house?" (Luke 2:49). At twelve, Jesus was already fulfilling David's prophecy, "Zeal for Your house has consumed me" (Ps. 69:9). I think of the exhilaration of Jesus, a young boy who was grasping truth and consciousness of great things, great purpose, and great identity. As we contemplate Jesus and the Scriptures, let's think of our own grasp of truth, great things, purpose and identity. We will see how the Bible deals with some of these issues in relation to being united to Christ and living his likeness.

YOUNG JESUS AND THE SCRIPTURES

Jesus "grew in wisdom and stature, and in favor with God and man" by reading and studying the Scriptures (See Luke 2:52). Like most Jewish boys, at five, Jesus probably started studying and memorizing the five books of Moses, the Torah. All the years of hiding God's Word in his heart as a child kept Jesus from sin. He was tempted in every way that we are (See Heb. 4:15), and yet he was the perfect example of the "young person" the psalmist speaks of in Psalm 119:9–11 (New Living Translation).

> How can a young person stay pure?
>> By obeying your word.
> I have tried hard to find you—
>> don't let me wander from your commands.
> I have hidden your word in my heart,
>> that I might not sin against you.

What words of wisdom for each of us, even if we're not a young person! Obey the Word! Seek God! Ask for God's help to keep his commands! Hide his Word in your heart to keep from sin! Treasuring the Word with all our heart like young Jesus keeps us from sinning against God by understanding his love and grace. Even here in the Old Testament there is the exhortation to "stay pure" the way God is pure.

SUPREMACY OF JESUS' WORDS

The Bible says that in the beginning, the Word was with God and was God (John 1:1). Jesus was the Word and came to earth to reveal his Father's mind in a similar way that our words reveal the thoughts of our mind. "And the Word became flesh and dwelt among us, and we have seen his glory, glory as of the only Son from the Father, full of grace and truth" (John 1:14). Even at creation the plan was for Jesus to demonstrate the glorious truth of God, in person, to those he created. The Scriptures that we have today in our Bible will stand because they contain the very thoughts and words of God. Before Jesus came and throughout his ministry, the written revelation of God to the world was through the Old Testament. These Scriptures were vital to Jesus and his mission on earth, which ultimately was to reconcile us to God and show us how to live pure lives. Jesus often referred to Old Testament Scriptures in his three-year ministry. His reference to and reverence for the Scriptures is an example for his followers to also know and revere them.

God declared that the words of Jesus as spoken and reported, are the new way God communicates to those on earth. The writer of Hebrews beautifully expresses it this way: "Long ago, at many times and in many ways, God spoke to our fathers by the prophets, but in these last days he has spoken to us by his Son" (Heb. 1:1 ESV). John says in his gospel, "No one has ever seen God, but the one and only Son, who is Himself God and is at the Father's side, has made Him known" (1:18). It reminds me of a possible news headline— Jesus Reports the Latest from God! Jesus accurately communicates his Father's image and character to the world with both words and actions. In multiple New Testament passages Jesus accepts his role as speaker for God. Jesus says:

> Do you not believe that I am in the Father and the Father is in Me? The words I say to you, I do not speak on My own. Instead, it is the Father dwelling in Me, performing His works (John 14:10).
>
> Whoever does not love Me does not keep My words. The word that you hear is not My own, but it is from the Father who sent Me (John 14:24). [The opposite is true also: whoever loves Me keeps My words.]

We learn here the great humility of Jesus who gives God credit for his message, and also the double importance of what he says because they are the words of God spoken through the Son who is declaring that he repeats exactly what his Father says. How can we not see the importance and the truth of what Jesus said and how he reveals the Father in the Bible?

JESUS' TEMPTATION IN THE WILDERNESS

Traveling to Israel and walking in places where Jesus walked is a life-changing event, but the fact that we know the actual words Jesus spoke is even more remarkable and valuable; he is the Word made flesh who came to dwell with us (John 1:14). Sometimes we struggle to find time to read the Bible, or we might hear, "I just don't get much out of the Old Testament." Jesus was steeped in the study of the Old Testament Scriptures, and we have his example to follow. The Scriptures he often quoted were from the Torah or Pentateuch written by Moses, and the prophets such as Isaiah and David. In the book of Daniel, the heavenly messenger that came to Daniel said he would tell him what is in the "Book of Truth" (See Dan. 10:10–21). The Book of Truth revealed to Daniel prophesies about Jesus who is the way, the truth, and the life.

In the secular world, we say knowledge is power. The same is true in the spiritual world. Knowledge of the Word of God is power. Jesus, fully God but fully man, was subject to temptation as we are. Because he knew the Scriptures and spent time in prayer with his Father, he had the knowledge, wisdom, and power to overcome sin and temptation. Jesus, the perfect man, was finally the perfect priest to represent us to God. Hebrews 4:15 says, "For we do not have a high priest who is unable to sympathize with our weaknesses, but we have one who was tempted in every way that we are, yet was without sin."

At the beginning of his ministry, Jesus was baptized by John, and then fasted forty days and forty nights in the wilderness, most likely being tempted by Satan throughout all those days (Luke 4:2). Jesus used three Scriptures from Deuteronomy 6 and 8 to strike down Satan's final three assaults to bring him to counter God's will. Let's look at Jesus' example of rejecting Satan's temptations, taken from Matthew 4:3–11 (ESV).

> Satan: "If you are the Son of God, command these stones to become loaves of bread."
> Jesus: "It is written, 'Man shall not live by bread alone, but by every word that comes from the mouth of God.'" (See Eze. 20:11 also—source of life.)
>
> Satan: "If you are the Son of God, throw yourself down [from the pinnacle of the temple], for it is written, 'He will

command his angels concerning you,' and 'On their hands they will bear you up, lest you strike your foot against a stone.'" [Satan extra devious here quoting Scripture himself!] Jesus: "Again it is written, 'You shall not put the Lord your God to the test.'"

Satan: "All these [kingdoms of the world] I will give you, if you will fall down and worship me." [See Ps. 2:8 for God's promise to his Son. Satan surely knew this.]
Jesus: "Be gone, Satan! For it is written, 'You shall worship the Lord your God and him only shall you serve.'"

I love the defense, "Be gone, Satan! For it is written. . . . " It could be used against Satan many times a day by one who knows the Scriptures. Jesus even exclaimed to Peter, "Get behind me, Satan!" when Peter rebuked Jesus for saying he would go to Jerusalem and be killed. It was an offense to Jesus because Peter was not setting his mind on the things of God, but on the things of men (See Matt. 16:22–23).

Responding to temptation with "It is written," like Jesus, overcomes every temptation or circumstance in life if we know the Scripture and use God-given wisdom in applying it. The Holy Spirit, the Spirit of Jesus, in the life of the believer imparts love for and understanding of the Word of God which in turn serves to guard and protect from the constant attacks of Satan.

JESUS TEACHES THE IMPORTANCE OF SCRIPTURE

The Pharisees, Sadducees, and Herodians were usually at odds with each other, but they all agreed that Jesus was a threat to them and their religious beliefs, so they mounted joint theological attacks against him. Let's look at one exchange, which is recorded in three gospels, which shows how important it was. The Sadducees came and asked Jesus who would be the husband in heaven for a woman who had been married to seven brothers, one after the other, each of which had died, and then she died. This is a far-fetched scenario, but the Sadducees felt this would be a good way to prove believing in resurrection was foolishness. Jesus answered them and said, "You are mistaken because you do not know the Scriptures, nor the power of God" (Matt. 22:29).

Who would want Jesus to say that to them? If the Sadducees had really believed the Old Testament Scriptures, they would have seen that atonement and salvation with eternal life, were to be provided by All-Powerful God. They would have known salvation meant there would be a resurrection. Jesus addresses their disbelief by asking them, "And as for the resurrection of the dead, have you not read what was said to you by God: 'I am the God of Abraham, and the God of Isaac, and the God of Jacob'? He is not the God of the dead, but of the living" (Matt. 22:31–32). First, Jesus asks, "Have you not read . . . ?" He knew they had read and probably memorized this from Exodus 3:6 but had not understood the importance of the present tense, "I am the God…." God did not say, "I was the God." When Jesus questions them, he makes it clear that it was God himself speaking through Moses and now to the Sadducees, even though the words were spoken over 1,000 years earlier. God is speaking to each of us individually today as well. What can we learn? We have the responsibility of understanding what God has said and the power of his words.

Alexander MacLaren described the Sadducees' challenge to Jesus in this eloquent way: "Their questions were cunningly contrived to entangle Him in the cobwebs of [religious doctrine] and theological hairsplitting, but He walked through the fine-spun snares as a lion might stalk away with the nooses set for him dangling behind him."[10] Jesus was never defined by man or defeated in a theological argument. The Sadducees and Pharisees did not understand it is in the spirit of the law, not the letter of the law, that God gives full meaning and revelation. Through the Bible, the Holy Spirit speaks his truth to the reader across the years from the time of Moses until today. No other book is like the

Bible, with the Holy Spirit present to burn into hearts the truth and blessing in what is read.

After his death and resurrection, Jesus had an encounter or more likely an appointment, with two men who had been mourning and weeping with other disciples of Jesus. They knew that Jesus' body had disappeared from the tomb, but when Mary Magdalene came to those who had gathered to mourn Jesus and said she had seen him and he was alive, they did not believe her (Mark 16:11). Two of these men were traveling into the country toward Emmaus, about a seven-mile walk from Jerusalem, when Jesus appeared to them as they walked. They did not recognize him, so when he asked why they were sad, they told him about Jesus of Nazareth, a prophet, being crucified and his body disappearing. At that point, Jesus exclaimed, "O foolish and slow of heart to believe in all that the Prophets have spoken. Was it not necessary for the Christ to suffer these things and to come into His glory?" He began to explain to them what Moses and all the prophets had written about him, including his death and return to heaven. It was not until Jesus broke bread with them, blessed it, and gave it to them, that their eyes were opened, and they realized the Messiah himself was sharing a meal with them. The Bible says he disappeared, and the men, thinking back to their time together on the road, said, "Were not our hearts burning within us . . . as he opened the Scriptures to us?" (Taken from Luke 24).

Contemplating His Ways:

Jesus at twelve was beginning a life of consecration to God and to his mission in life. How has that happened for you? How do you keep learning about God and your mission in life?

You may not be growing in stature anymore, but how can you grow in wisdom and favor with God and man like Jesus did?

Orthodox Jews show honor and respect for the Word of God by kissing it before and after opening the book and reading. How do you show reverence for the Word of God?

CHAPTER 4

RESPONDING TO THE WORD OF GOD

Whoever does [these commandments] and teaches them will be called great in the kingdom of heaven.—Jesus
MATTHEW 5:19B

After Jesus ate in Emmaus with the men who finally recognized him at the table, he vanished. These two men were so excited about seeing Jesus that they hurried back to Jerusalem that evening and told the disciples and others what had happened. As they were speaking, Jesus appeared in the room! There and in following days during Jesus' last hours on earth, Luke reveals some of what happened. We learn that the disciples heard him teach the truth about himself in the Old Testament; heard his promise of the Holy Spirit; watched in amazement as Jesus was taken up into heaven; worshipped him fervently; returned to Jerusalem with great joy; and gathered continually praising and blessing God (Luke 24:33–53).

How about today? Have you had a memorable experience of listening to a great, perhaps well-known Bible teacher or preacher that opened your eyes to great spiritual truths? I am thinking back to the 1960s when Billy Graham was in Kansas City. My church took a bus fifty miles to the big city. I don't remember Dr. Graham's message, maybe because I was distracted by a cute guy in our youth group, but I know it was a powerful call to believe in Jesus, and many people streamed down to the field when "Just as I Am" was sung.

It would have been wonderful to have heard Jesus teach in person, and yet we have access to the truth he taught and the Scriptures he loved right in the precious Bible. In his Turning Point devotion, David Jeremiah wrote, "When we get alone with God and open His Word, we're entering a nuclear reactor, a treasury building, a communications center, a vast library, an illumined chamber, a music hall, and a dear friend's house—all at once. All of that is in our 'closet.'" God's plan is clearly stated by Paul in Romans: "For everything that was written in the past was written for our instruction, so that through endurance and the encouragement of the Scriptures, we might have hope" (15:4). Just like the disciples of Jesus, we can respond to the words of God by listening to the Holy Spirit as we read the Scripture; believing in Jesus and following him; worshiping fervently and joyfully; and gathering continually praising and blessing God. Let's start back with Moses and see how the children of Israel responded to the reading of God's Word before entering the Promised Land. It is amazing that from the time of Moses through to the time of Jesus, and until today, the message and power of the Word of God continues. This consistent witness gives creditability to the truth of the Bible and to God as its ultimate author. We'll be looking at hearing, learning, obeying, and joyfully receiving the Word and the reward of God in the pages to come.

HEARING THE WORD OF GOD

Whoever belongs to God hears the words of God.—Jesus
JOHN 8:47

In the Hebrew language, the Feast of Tabernacles is called *Sukkot*, the word for booths or tents. Jews have celebrated this feast since it was commanded by God as written in Leviticus 23, about 3,500 years ago. It is celebrated in Israel every fall after the somber festival of *Yom Kippur* when Jews fast, repent for sins committed over the past year, and ask God for forgiveness. Everything grinds to a halt during *Yom Kippur;* TV and radio broadcasting stops, and public transportation including buses and airports are closed down. Young people enjoy riding bikes or skateboarding on normally busy highways, which are empty of cars on that day. The unity and solidarity of the Israeli people on this day and all feast days is surprising for us who live in a larger, more diverse, and often divided society.

Gears change quickly when *Sukkot* arrives five days after Yom Kippur. It is a joyful holiday for remembering God's salvation, shelter, and provision for his people in the wilderness after leading them out of slavery in Egypt. Jews build a *sukkah* which is a three or four-sided small room in open air, covered by branches and leaves. Families decorate these shelters, which commemorate the tents the children of Israel lived in during their wilderness wanderings. Families eat their meals and many sleep in the *sukkah*. An important part of the holiday is the reading of the Torah scrolls, which are paraded in the synagogue with joyous singing and dancing.

Before entering the Promised Land after forty years in the wilderness, Moses commanded the priests and elders to gather the people of all ages during Sukkot, the Feast of Tabernacles, to hear the reading of the law.

> Assemble the people—men, women, children, and the foreigners within your gates —so that they may listen [*hear,* ESV] and *learn* to fear the LORD your God and to *follow* carefully all the words of this law. Then their children who do not know the law will listen and learn to fear the LORD your God, as long as you live in the land that you are crossing the Jordan to possess (Deut. 31:12–13 emphasis mine).

Moses' call was for the Israelites to hear, learn, and follow the Word of God in the Promised Land that they would soon enter. Knowing how the children of Israel had rebelled against God's commandments in the wilderness, his call was as much a warning as instruction. We can take the call to hear, learn, and follow in the same way. In our culture, "hearing" includes reading since unlike when the Bible was written; we have easy access to the text and have the ability to read it ourselves.

TEACHING OUR CHILDREN

Teaching our children the Word of God is a priority often repeated in the Bible. We have already seen Moses including the little ones, who sadly had not known about God, in the reading of the law before entering the Promised Land. He said they are to hear and learn to worship and follow God. The parents are to teach the words of God "diligently to your children and speak of them when you sit at home and when you walk along the road, when you lie down and when you get up. Tie them as reminders on your hands and bind them on your foreheads. Write them on the doorposts of your houses and on your gates" (Deut. 6:7–9). The idea is that the words of God are to be so dominant in the lives of these children that everywhere they turn they are reminded of the greatness of God and that they are to "love the LORD your God with all your heart and with all your soul and with all your strength" (Deut. 6:5).

Jews and many Christians in Israel take the command to write God's commands on the doorposts of their houses quite literally and have a scroll containing the words of Deuteronomy 6:4-9 inside a small box called a *mezuzah* attached to the doorpost of their house. *Mezuzah* in Hebrew is "doorpost," the word used in the Deuteronomy 6 passage. Printed on the outside of the box is the Hebrew letter *shin* (שׁ), the first letter of the word shema, or Hear! in English, which is the first word on the passage inside. The *shin* is also printed on the back of the little scroll along with two other letters that are the initials for the Hebrew words meaning "Guardian of the doors of Israel." The same three letters also spell one of God's names—*Shaddai*. What a great reminder on the doorpost: take God's command for our families seriously![11]

HEARING JESUS

A modern-day secular Israeli Jew has described Judaism as a religion based on obeying rules. There are 613 rules, he points out, including the well-known Ten Commandments, but he notes that thousands more have been added by rabbis through the years. The 613 laws come from the Torah, which in the view of Christian followers of Jesus are so much more than books of rules. Along with the New Testament, these Old Testament Scriptures contain great revelation about the nature of God and his laws and precepts that are life giving. John, a beloved disciple and eyewitness to the ministry of Jesus, wrote, "The law was given through Moses; grace and truth came through Jesus Christ" (John 1:17). Much more than a religion of rules, Christianity is about the God of the universe sending his Son, full of grace and truth, to give life in place of death.

George Muller was a man who learned the richness of the Word of Christ. He was a minister who founded a large orphanage complex in England in the mid-1800s that served 2,000 orphans over 25 years. He determined to do all this work with donations that were given without his asking for anything. He relied on God to supply every need, and God did. At times there was not enough food but through earnest prayer, God provided what they needed. Muller also gave away more than 250,000 Bibles. In later years, he visited 42 countries, preaching and urging people to read their Bibles, pray, and rely on God. In later years, it was his practice to read through the entire Bible four times a year.[12] In May of 1841, Muller wrote that he had learned how important it was to be nourished and strengthened in the inner man day by day in order to do acts of service for the Lord. He had during a period of his life spent much time in prayer each morning, but as he expressed it:

> Now, I saw that the most important thing I had to do was to give myself to the reading of the word of God, and to meditation on it, that thus my heart might be comforted,

encouraged, warned, reproved, instructed; and that thus, by means of the word of God, while meditating on it, my heart might be brought into . . . communion with the Lord. . . . For when it pleased the Lord in August 1829 to bring me really to the Scriptures, my life and walk became very different. And though ever since that I have very much fallen short of what I might and ought to be, yet by the grace of God I have been enabled to live much nearer to Him than before. If any believers read this who practically prefer other books to the Holy Scriptures, and who enjoy the writings of men much more than the word of God, may they be warned by my loss. The frequent reading of the Scriptures creates a delight in them, so that the more we read them, the more we desire to do so.[13]

George Muller's faith came from, as he said, his "communion with the Lord," based on much meditation on the Word of God. The stories of so many Bible characters, like Abraham, Joseph, Moses, the widow of Zarephath, Rehab of Jericho, Gideon, and others, illustrate God's miracles of provision and protection. All of us can learn the character of God when "hearing" the Scriptures, leading to rely on God to be faithful just as he was to so many we read about in the Bible today.

Contemplating His Ways:

Have you experienced the Bible as a nuclear reactor, a treasury building, a communications center, a vast library, an illumined chamber, a music hall, and a dear friend's house? How could that be?

RESPONDING TO THE WORD OF GOD

Have you ever felt that Christianity was a bunch of rules? How do we know that's not true?

George Muller said to be warned by his own experience of loss when he preferred the writings of men to the Word of God. What would happen if that were reversed for our lives?

CHAPTER 5

WONDERS OF THE WORD

Open my eyes that I may see wondrous things from Your law.
PSALM 119:18

LEARNING THE WORDS OF GOD

Do you have memories of a long-time, faithful Sunday school teacher, who taught Sunday school for years and years, sacrificing time and energy week after week to teach young ones about God? My daughters had a wonderful, faithful teacher in our church in Vancouver, Washington who taught for twenty-five years, Sunday after Sunday. I admired her and marveled at her love for kids and for the Lord. Her reward in heaven, and legacy on earth, are great.

Psalm 71:18 says that the goal of the aged is to "proclaim Your power to the next generations, Your might to all who are to come." By the time we are aged, we should have collected and passed on many examples of God's power and might! Because of the importance of teaching the Scriptures to younger generations, we ourselves must seek to understand the Bible. The Holy Spirit is our greatest teacher when we read the word of God. In John we read, "But the Advocate, the Holy Spirit, whom the Father will send in My name, will teach you all things and will remind you of everything I have told you" (14:26). We saw how George Muller discovered by experience that the most important thing for him was: "to give myself to the reading of the word of God, and to meditate on it."

Pray for the desire and ability to see the hand of God and understand his wondrous works both in the Bible and in your world. The writer of Psalm 119 said, "The unfolding of Your words gives light; it informs the simple" (v. 130). There are no qualifications for seeing this light and understanding the words in the Scriptures. God desires that all people should know him and be saved from sin and death. Reading the Bible is meant to be a conversation with God through the Spirit of Jesus. There is more depth and meaning in each passage, sentence, word, and even letter than we can understand on our human level, but the living, powerful, active word of God speaks to us the truth we need for the moment when we are open to the voice of the Holy Spirit.

Jesus' last teaching was with his disciples after he returned from walking to Emmaus with the two of his followers. During that walk he explained what was written about him in the Old Testament. It was such a powerful message that the hearts of his two companions burned as he was speaking.

Jesus returned to Jerusalem that night and began to teach his disciples. Luke tells us in chapter 24 (vv. 44–45) what he said to them: "These are the words I spoke to you while I was still with you: Everything must be fulfilled that is written about Me in the Law of Moses, the Prophets, and the Psalms. Then He opened their minds to understand the Scriptures." This must have been a summary of his presence throughout the history of the whole world, including his presence in the Old Testament, beginning with Genesis. How I hope to hear it someday! It must have been such a revelation to the disciples to see how Jesus was present in the Law of Moses, the Prophets, and the Psalms. It opens a fascinating area of study for today.

After his teaching, Jesus told the disciples to stay in Jerusalem because he was sending the "Promise of My Father," the Holy Spirit, who would fill them "with power from on high" (v. 49). Jesus said the Holy

Spirit will give us power, teach us all things, and remind us of all things that he said!

Did you notice Jesus taught his disciples about himself in the Old Testament? This is an example of how we should read the Bible, looking for what it teaches us about the three persons of the Trinity. Bible professor and author, Kristi McLelland gives great insight into reading the Bible through what she calls the "Middle Eastern lens." After all, the Bible is written by Middle Easterners with their own cultural views and setting in contrast to our Western culture. When we Westerners read the Bible, we tend to want to understand how something happened or what it looked like and then we will believe. The Middle Eastern mind tends to say, "God, I believe you: I take you at your word. Out of my belief, provide me with understanding."

Instead of saying, "What happened?" a Middle Eastern question might be, "Why did God do that?" McLelland gives the example of the book of Jonah. What was it about? A reluctant prophet and a big fish? No, it was about God loving evil people and sending his prophet to tell them about him. When we focus on learning about God, we gaze at him in the Scriptures instead of looking at ourselves and asking what does this teach me about myself? McLelland writes, "As we gaze at Him, we will be changed from the inside out." Isn't that what we want? To be more like him.[14]

God has sent his Holy Spirit to burn into our hearts the very image of Jesus when we read and meditate on his Word. Psalm 14:2 says, "The LORD looks down from heaven upon the sons of men to see if any understand, if any seek God." Jesus calls us today to understand and recognize him in the Scriptures, and to believe he is the Messiah. The gospel of Jesus the Christ was foretold in Old Testament Scripture, repeated by Jesus to all who followed him, and recorded in the New Testament. What the prophets could only see in the future, we see fulfilled in Jesus. One of these prophets, Hosea, said, "My people are destroyed for lack of knowledge.... So a people without understanding will come to ruin" (Hos. 4:6,14). Hosea's warning came 700 years before Jesus told his companions traveling to Emmaus not to be slow of heart to believe what the prophets such as Hosea had spoken. There is amazing consistency of this Bible message: we should not be foolish, slow of heart to believe, destroyed for lack of knowledge, or ruined due to lack of understanding the Word of God.[15]

UNDERSTANDING THE WORD OF GOD

Archeologists in Israel often find multiple layers of civilization at one dig representing thousands of years of human occupation. What appears at the surface is only one layer of civilized life. For example, Tel Megiddo has 30 layers of civilization, one built on top of the other, forming a *tel*, or hill. Similarly, a verse, a passage, or a story from the Bible has many different layers of meaning depending on who is reading it and at what point in their life. The same verse could have a new meaning and give understanding according to your season of life. God uses his Word to speak to you when you have an open heart. The writer of Hebrews 4:12 put it this way: "For the word of God *is* living and powerful, and sharper than any two-edged sword, piercing even to the division of soul and spirit, and of joints and marrow, and is a discerner of the thoughts and intents of the heart" (NKJ). The Bible is much more than a history book because it is "living and powerful."

Paul told Timothy that knowledge of the Word of God was like treasure entrusted to him. In a traditional treasure hunt, there is no guarantee of finding treasure. However, we are guaranteed to find treasure when we study the Word of God! Let's look at Psalm 119 to illustrate this treasure. With a little research there are discoveries to be uncovered in this beautiful psalm where the theme is well-represented by the seventy-second verse: "The law from Your mouth is more precious to me than thousands of pieces of gold and silver" (Ps. 119:72).

The entire chapter celebrates the perfection of the laws of God, which are also called precepts, commandments, words, testimonies, decrees, and statutes in the psalm. David Powlison said in his book *Speaking the*

Truth in Love, "Psalm 119 is the thoughtful outcry that rises when real life meets real God." Psalm 119:71 is a good illustration of real life and needing real God: "It is good for me to be afflicted, that I might learn your statutes." Going through difficult times is an opportunity to learn more about God and his faithfulness in the midst of trouble.

Psalm 119 is an acrostic poem. It has been suggested that the acrostic organization is a demonstration of the perfection of God and his law. There is one eight-line stanza dedicated to each of the twenty-two letters of the Hebrew alphabet beginning with *aleph* and ending with *taw*. Each line of the eight-line stanzas begins with the particular letter of the Hebrew alphabet that is being used. I have found this psalm to be fascinating! During my devotions one morning I was reading Psalm 119:25-32, which is the fourth stanza for the fourth Hebrew letter, *daleth* ד. The most noticeable theme is the word, statutes, precepts, works, testimonies, and commandments of God, all words used within these eight lines.

The first thing that struck me in this stanza was Psalm 119:26, "I have declared my ways, and You answered me; Teach me Your statutes" (NKJV). When we talk to God, we can expect him to answer! We tell him what is going on and he answers, sometimes simply by showing us our answer in the Bible. Then, I noticed the word "way" was repeated in five of the eight lines in the stanza. I also saw "truth," "revive me," "strengthen me," and "You shall enlarge my heart." Putting it together you see references to Jesus, who is the way, the truth, and the life presented here in the Old Testament psalm!

This was an exciting discovery, but I knew I had to look further, so I used a parallel study Bible comparing the English verse with the Hebrew verse.[16] I was looking for what the Hebrew words were that the poet used at the beginning of each of the eight lines for this fourth stanza, all beginning with the letter *daleth*. If you have written a poem, you understand the challenges. You sit and search for just the right word because the language, sounds, and rhythms must be melded with your meaning. It is intriguing to think of the struggles the writer of Psalm 119 had with his

Hebrew language. After all, how hard would it be to try eight meaningful lines all starting with X in our English alphabet?

What I found was that only three different words beginning with the Hebrew letter *daleth* were used and repeated at the beginning of all eight, Lines 25–32: *dabaq*, *derek*, and *dalaph*. Here are their meanings:

25 dabaq: to cling, keep close
26 derek: way, road, manner
27 derek: way, road, manner
28 dalaph: drip, drop
29 derek: way, road, manner
30 derek: way, road, manner
31 dabaq: cling, keep close
32 derek: way, road, manner

I like to think the use of *derek* and *dabaq* gives emphasis to "clinging" to the "way," of Jesus. I hope you will stick with me because there is one more connection I want to point out. Each Hebrew letter has a name, sometimes associated with its shape, adding an extra dimension of meaning, which can meld, with meaning of the text where it is used. The name of the fourth letter itself, *daleth*, is related to the word "door." Jesus said, "I am the door of the sheep." This relates to the emphasis on "the way" in these verses. In the context of the Hebrew alphabet, this letter also symbolizes a person's heart, which, like a door, can be either closed or open to God.[17] In fact, the last line, Verse 32 is translated, "I will run the way of thy commandments, when thou shalt enlarge my heart" (KJV).

These word associations beautifully tie the name of the letter *daleth* with the theme of the *daleth* stanza. Considering how amazing and wonderful our God is, it shouldn't be a surprise to find such treasures in his Word; it is intriguing to know there are more astounding discoveries yet to be made!

Contemplating His Ways:

Does the Word of God seem living and powerful to you? How does it become that way?

How can reading the Bible be a conversation between you and God?

What are some places we see Jesus in the Old Testament? This is a fascinating study that reveals more about the person of Jesus.

CHAPTER 6

DOING AND DELIGHTING IN THE WORD

*Be doers of the word, and not hearers only.
Otherwise, you are deceiving yourselves*
JAMES 1:22

BEING DOERS OF THE WORD

Mark Twain was a skeptic when it came to Christianity. Traveling in the Holy Land in 1867, he wrote, Israel is "monotonous and uninviting.... It is a hopeless, dreary, heart-broken land.... [a] desolate country whose soil is rich enough, but is given over wholly to weeds—a silent mournful expanse.... A desolation is here that not even imagination can grace with the pomp of life and action.... We never saw a human being on the whole route.... There was hardly a tree or a shrub anywhere. Even the olive and the cactus, those fast friends of the worthless soil, had almost deserted the country."[18]

Twain saw no splendor in the Holy Land. He wrote rather irreverently about the country's holiest sites. The Sea of Galilee was "a solemn, sailless, tintless lake, as unpoetical as any bath-tub on earth." The Church of the Nativity [in Bethlehem] was "tricked out in the usual tasteless style observable in all the holy places of Palestine."[19]

My description of the land of Israel is totally different. I saw olive trees everywhere, lined along steep, terraced hills. Covered banana plantations with huge bunches of bananas bagged in bright blue spilled down toward the Sea of Galilee, near the site of the Sermon on the Mount. Groves of date palms lined the highways in the desert by the Dead Sea where industries harvest valuable minerals. Clusters of bright white homes and apartment buildings dotted the hills around Jerusalem. The busy airport and public transportation served the bustling cities.

Why was Israel so desolate in Twain's day? God declares in the ninth chapter of Jeremiah that Jerusalem, will become "a heap of rubble, a haunt for jackals; and . . . the cities of Judah a desolation, without inhabitant" (v. 11). Then Jeremiah speaks to God and asks, "Who is wise enough to understand this, and explain why the land is destroyed and scorched so that no one can pass through it?" (v. 12, author's paraphrase).

God answers, "It is because they have forsaken My law, which I set before them; they have not walked in it or obeyed My voice" (v. 13). There are plenty of eyewitnesses who saw the fulfillment of this prophecy of destruction of the land of Israel over the 1,800 years that the Jews were scattered among the nations, driven out by God because of forsaking his law and worshiping other gods.

Why is the land of Israel so productive and flourishing today? This too is fulfillment of prophecy and God's blessing. True to God's Word, the Jews, who continue to return to their land today, are sowing fields, planting vineyards, and yielding a fruitful harvest. You can see with your eyes the fulfillment of Ezekiel 36:35: "Then they will say, 'This land that was desolate has become like the garden of Eden.'"

God has restored Israel from captivity and given them the land and nation of Israel. He gave them these promises before they entered the Promised Land:

> When all these things come upon you—the blessings
> and curses I have set before you—and you call them to

mind in all the nations to which the Lord your God has banished you, and when you and your children return to the Lord your God and *obey His voice with all your heart and all your soul* according to everything I am giving you today, then He will restore you from captivity and have compassion on you and gather you from all the nations to which the Lord your God has scattered you.

So the Lord your God will make you abound in all the work of your hands and in the fruit of your womb, the offspring of your livestock, and the produce of your land. Indeed, the Lord will again delight in your goodness, as He delighted in that of your fathers, if you obey the Lord your God by keeping His commandments and statutes that are written in this Book of the Law, and if you *turn to Him with all your heart and with all your soul* (Deuteronomy 30:1-3, 9-10, emphasis mine).

What did Jesus say about obeying the Word of God? God's commandment written by Moses did not change. Jesus repeated it and it is for us today: "*'Love the Lord your God with all your heart and with all your soul and with all your mind.' This is the first and greatest commandment*" (Matt. 22:37–40, emphasis mine). He also said, "If you love Me, you will keep My commandments" (John 14:15). Loving God and obeying his commandments means loving Jesus and obeying his commandments.

DELIGHTING IN THE WORD

Your testimonies are my heritage forever,
for they are the joy of my heart.
PSALM 119:111

God wants us to experience joy in hearing and understanding his Word. Ezra began a revival by reading the Book of the Law of Moses, which had been neglected for hundreds of years. The children of Israel had seen God's hand enabling them to rebuild the walls of Jerusalem. They wept when they realized they had not kept the law but had violated it and were in danger of judgment. There is place for that repentance, but because it was a holy day to be celebrated, Nehemiah, Ezra, and the Levite teachers urged them to rejoice when they heard the law, telling them not to mourn, because the joy of the Lord was their strength (See Nehemiah 8:10).

David writes of the joy and love he finds in the Word of God.

> The Law of the LORD is *perfect*,
> reviving the soul;
> the testimony of the LORD is *trustworthy*,
> making wise the simple.
> The precepts of the LORD are *right*,
> bringing joy to the heart;
> the commandments of the LORD are *radiant*,
> giving light to the eyes.
> The fear of the LORD is *pure*,
> enduring forever;
> the judgments of the LORD are *true*,
> being altogether righteous.
> They are more *precious* than gold,
> than much pure gold;
> they are *sweeter than honey*,
> than honey from the comb.
> By them indeed Your servant is warned;
> in keeping them is great reward (Ps. 19:7–11, emphasis mine).

God desires that we love and obey his law like David did. David sees the beauty of God's commands and the great reward for those who keep them.

He pens exhilarating praise to the great treasure of the Scriptures: the law, testimony, precepts, commands, and judgments of God; in other words, all that teaches the truth of God. His truth is perfect, trustworthy, right, radiant, pure, true, precious, and sweeter than honey from the honeycomb.

If we say yes to God, Psalm 19 tells us the result is:

- Our soul is revived.
- The simple is made wise.
- Our heart is joyful.
- There is light (understanding) in our eyes.
- We will forever exalt the Lord.
- We follow the righteous way.
- We possess a treasure like much pure gold.
- We enjoy the sweetness of the instruction of God.
- The warnings protect us.
- There is great reward in following the righteous way.

You can understand how the heart of the poet is so joyful when he speaks of God's Word here, which is full of abundance and richness in the revelation of his will. God wants us to be joyful! His treasure is the fruit of his righteousness and the love he has for those who love and follow him.

Israel was united in the days of King David and his son, King Solomon, but the kingdom was divided in the days of the prophet Isaiah, who prophesied in the southern kingdom of Judah to a people following in the sinful ways of the northern kingdom of Israel. Assyria conquered the northern kingdom, and Isaiah warned Judah of their own coming judgment by Babylon even before it became an empire and powerful threat. The people were consulting the spirits of the dead through mediums as a guide for living. Isaiah asks, "When men tell you to consult the spirits of the dead and the spiritists who whisper and mutter, shouldn't a people consult their God instead? Why consult the dead on behalf of the living?

To the law and to the testimony! If they do not speak according to this word, they have no light of dawn" (Is. 8:19–20).

Today, as in the day of Isaiah, only the Word of God is worthy to be followed; not the word of family, a particular spiritual leader, a politician, an inspirational speaker or author, or anyone you are invited to have confidence in. They may have insights if they truly know God and his Word, but the "light of dawn" is to be found in the Scriptures without fail. What a great promise! "Shouldn't a people seek their God?" Isaiah said. Isaiah knew God would hear and answer any plea for wisdom, knowledge, or direction. He is the one we can always trust.

The next chapter in Isaiah has the beautiful prophecy of the Messiah's birth, which is the remedy for the darkness spoken of in the previous chapter: "In the latter time he has made glorious the way of the sea, the land beyond the Jordan, Galilee of the nations. The people who walked in darkness have seen a great light; those who dwelt in a land of deep darkness, on them has light shone" (9:1b-2). This is such a wonderful way to describe the coming of Jesus to Galilee and to each of us wherever we are. We are in darkness without his marvelous light and without his Word. Isaiah continues in the next verses to describe the coming of Jesus. He will increase the joy of the nation that will rejoice in him like the rejoicing at harvest time or at a victory over enemies.

Now let's turn to the twentieth century. Evan Roberts, like David or Isaiah, loved the Word of God. He valued his Bible above anything else he had. He carried it wherever he went, including into the coal mine where he worked from the age of 12. He would take his Bible to work and put it in a convenient nook, ready to snatch a moment or two when he could to scan the pages he loved. This young man became a leader of the Welsh Revival from 1904 to 1905, which saw 100,000 converts over a period of six months. It was based on prayer and praise, especially in song. In a vivid report, one newspaper reporter wrote about one of the revival meetings.

The enthusiasm was unbounded. Women sang . . . and men jumped up one after the other to testify. One told in quivering accents the story of a drunken life. A working collier [coal miner] spoke like a practiced orator, and one can imagine what a note the testimony of a converted gypsy woman struck when, dressed in her best, she told of her reformation and repentance. . . . The latest convert is a policeman, who, after complaining that the people had gone mad after religion, so that there was nothing to do, went to see for himself, and bursting into tears, confessed the error of his way and repented."[20]

How Evan Roberts must have loved the Scriptures! God used him in a mighty way to share the joy of the salvation message to these souls who experienced the outpouring of the Holy Spirit. A memorial marking the fiftieth anniversary of the revival was placed at Moriah Chapel, the home church of Roberts. On the back of the column are these words:

Dear Friend,
God loves you. Therefore seek Him diligently, Pray to Him earnestly. Read His Word constantly.
Yours in the Gospel
Evan Roberts

This simple yet powerful message touches my heart—it comes across the years from a man who modeled love for God and his Word and brought people to their knees before God.

When we read God's Word constantly as Evan Roberts advised, it becomes the lamp for our feet and light for our path. The path of life becomes clear. It is the path of Jesus' footsteps (Ps. 85:13). As Paul said in 2 Corinthians, "But thanks be to God, who always leads us in Christ's triumphal procession and through us spreads the aroma of the knowledge of him in every place" (2:14 CSB). In the next chapter we will see how being "in Christ," in union with him, is why we are part of his triumphal procession, have his fragrance, and the true knowledge of him.

Contemplating His Ways:

How do you teach your children about the Bible?

George Muller said, "The frequent reading of the Scriptures creates a delight in them, so that the more we read them, the more we desire to do so." Has this been true for you? If not, how do you make that happen?

Paul wrote to the Colossians, "Let the word of Christ richly dwell in you" (3:16). We go through different seasons and experiences in our lives. Each one of them God understands and has a message for us. It is so critical to spend time in the Word to have the foundation for spiritual truth in each season. It is a living and active Word. It will have the answer, be encouragement, and bring peace and rest. It will show God's path to follow for that time. Think of a season in your life when you found what you needed in the Word of God. What do you need today?

PART TWO

UNION *with* JESUS *in the* BIBLE

In Part Two we will look at what the Bible says about spiritual connection, or union with Jesus that gives us all we need to live his likeness! We will trust the reliability of the Bible in revealing this truth. Arthur W. Pink said, "It is not sufficient to think of God as He may be conceived of in our imagination, instead, our thoughts of Him must be formed by what He has revealed of Himself in His word."[1]

Starting with an introduction to union, we will then look at Paul's message about union; how Jesus spoke about union; and the spiritual nature of union. I'm excited to share with you what I have discovered in the Bible about this union we have with God through redemption in Jesus and by his Holy Spirit. There is much joy and confidence that comes with living in him and he in us.

CHAPTER 7

UNITED WITH JESUS

Since you have accepted Christ Jesus as Lord,
live in union with him.
COLOSSIANS 2:6 (GNT)

He who unites himself with the Lord is one with Him in spirit.
1 CORINTHIANS 6:17

Paul wrote the verses above to the Colossians and the Corinthians. He is regarded as one of the most influential Christian missionaries and Bible authors of the first century. A zealous Pharisee, he was one in a thousand chosen to study under Gamaliel, a rabbi who belonged to a family that had served as chief rabbis for over 300 years. Under Gamaliel, Paul learned the Hebrew Scriptures of the Old Testament, and great dedication to the God of Moses. He became a murderous enemy of Jesus and persecutor of his followers because he considered him to be an imposter. That was until Jesus himself spoke to him in a vision as he traveled to Damascus. Much later, Paul told the story of his conversion to King Agrippa.

> About noon, O king, as I was on the road, I saw a light
> from heaven, brighter than the sun, shining around me
> and my companions. We all fell to the ground, and I

heard a voice say to me in Hebrew, "Saul, Saul, why do you persecute Me? It is hard for you to kick against the goads."
"Who are You, Lord?" I asked.
"I am Jesus, whom you are persecuting," the Lord replied. "But get up and stand on your feet. For I have appeared to you to appoint you as a servant and as a witness of what you have seen from Me and what I will show you. I will rescue you from your own people and from the Gentiles. I am sending you to them to open their eyes, so that they may turn from darkness to light and from the power of Satan to God, that they may receive forgiveness of sins and an inheritance among those sanctified by faith in Me" (Acts 26:13–18).

Why did Jesus say that Paul was persecuting him in the passage above? After all, he was not throwing Jesus into prison! I have a feeling Paul knew right away what Jesus meant even though there was no way Paul could have physically persecuted Jesus who had been crucified, had risen, and then ascended to heaven. Now he was speaking to him from heaven! Here is a key to understanding the believer's union with Christ. Jesus thought of himself as so joined to his followers that their persecution was also his persecution. This is why he said, "I am Jesus, whom you are persecuting." In other words, when you persecute my followers who are joined to me, you are persecuting me.

What Paul wrote later helps explain what Jesus said: "He who unites himself with the Lord is one with Him in spirit" (1 Cor. 6:17). Let's read that again! We become one in spirit with Jesus when we put our faith in him. No wonder Jesus said Paul was persecuting him when he persecuted Christians. They were one in spirit with Jesus. Persecuting them was persecuting Jesus who was spiritually united to them. Here we see the beginning of our look into union with Christ.

The very beginning of this union goes all the way back before the world was made. Paul writes to the "saints" and "faithful *in Christ Jesus*" who are in Ephesus, "Blessed be the God and Father of our Lord Jesus Christ, who has blessed us with every spiritual blessing in the heavenly places *in Christ*, just as He chose us *in Him* before the foundation of the world, that we should be holy and without blame *before Him in love*" (Eph. 1:3–4 NKJV, emphasis mine; See also 2 Tim. 1:9). It is important to note that God blessed us "in Christ," and chose us for this loving union before the creation of the world. John Murray writes, "As far back as we can go in tracing salvation to its fountain we find 'union with Christ'; it is not something tacked on; it is there from the outset."[2]

Before we continue, let's stop and ask why God would choose anyone to live in union with him? There are answers in Ephesians 1 if we continue on. First of all, we see in the two verses above that God wants to bless us "in Christ" with "every spiritual blessing in the heavenly realms." Every spiritual blessing is very comprehensive! But why? Reading on we see it was in love that "He predestined us for adoption as His sons through Jesus Christ, according to the good pleasure of His will, to the praise of His glorious grace, which He has freely given us in the Beloved One" (1:4–6). It is because God loves us so much that he wants to unite with us through his Son. This love is like the love of a father for his children; it is the love of the God of the universe who was pleased to adopt children, sinful as they are, through the gift of "glorious grace" given in the Beloved One. Our part is to accept this gift and return the love as sons and daughters of God through faith in Jesus. Not only is love the genesis for adopting us as children but it also gives us opportunity to give praise to God for his glorious, freely given grace in providing our salvation through his Son.

We see the fountain of salvation beginning with many prophets in the Old Testament who looked for a savior redeemer. Job laments that he does not understand why God let him lose his family, wealth, and health. God seems like a judge who has condemned him even though in his mind he is not worthy of such fury. He mourns that God seems too powerful, too far away, and too unapproachable. "He is not a mere mortal like me that I might answer him, that we might confront each other in court. If only there were someone to mediate between us, someone to bring us together [lay his hand on us both, NKJV]" (Job 9:32–33 NIV). It turns out that this idea of a mediator with one hand on God and one hand on his created being, is a beautiful expression of the joining of God and man made possible through Jesus. It reminds me of God's hand reaching for man's, in Michelangelo's painting at the Sistine Chapel.

Don't you love the picture of a mediator, one hand on God, and the other hand on you? It is a picture of how Jesus made it possible to reconcile sinful men to a holy God. He humbled himself and came as a man, like the created ones that he and his Father chose to eternally love. Paul said, "There is one God, and there is one mediator between God and men, the man Christ Jesus" (1 Tim 2:5). Like Job, in our imperfection, we do not have access to the far away, unapproachable, all-powerful, holy God, but we can approach him through the Son of Man, Christ Jesus. Think of the humility and obedience of Jesus, who "made Himself of no reputation, taking the form of a bondservant, and coming in the likeness of men. He humbled Himself and became obedient to the point of death, even the death of the cross" (Phil. 2:7–8 NKJV). He took our sin upon himself, becoming the perfect and final sacrifice for sin. Only Jesus did that! All God's promises of blessing and nearness are made manifest in Jesus. Only our God did that!

God himself gave his Son to unite with those who accept the free gift of salvation. We become partakers of all it means to be *in Christ and Christ to be in us.* Jesus was made sin for us that we might be made the righteousness of God *in him* (2 Cor. 5:21). Then we are strengthened with power through his Spirit *in our inner being* (Eph. 3:16). What could be a more complete and blessed change of state than to be transformed *in him* and to have the Spirit of God *in us*? Christ is in us, and we are in Christ.

There are other unions that are key to understanding God's work: the union of God the Father, God the Son, and God the Holy Spirit, in the Trinity. Another is the union of the divine and human in Jesus when he came to earth. His Incarnation made a third union possible: union of Jesus, the Son of the living God, with those who believe in him.

Our union with Christ is only possible because Jesus came to earth to give his life to die in our place, keeping his divine nature but taking on human nature. "[He] was tempted in every way that we are, yet was without sin" (Heb. 4:15). Jesus knew what it was to rely on God. Jesus said, "I am in My Father" (John 14:20), which was why, as fully God and fully man, he was able to overcome temptation and live without sin, united with his Father. This is our goal, to live in union with Jesus. In John 14:20 Jesus added, "I am in My Father, and you are in Me, and I am in you."

When we are united to Jesus, we are also united with the Father because Jesus is in the Father. Through this union we enjoy the fullness and riches of God as we follow Jesus. When you read the Bible, especially the New Testament, you will find the theme of the life and Spirit of Christ in you, and you in Christ, throughout.

Let's stop here to consider. Have you been eternally united with the Lord by putting your faith in Jesus? My prayer is that everyone reading here about all the blessings of union with Christ, is truly united to him. When you believe in faith that Jesus, the Son of God, came to earth to take the punishment for your sins upon himself on the cross, you will be saved and receive his life. John 3:16 says this simply and powerfully: "For God so loved the world, that He gave His only Son, so that everyone who believes in Him will not perish, but have eternal life" (NASB).

Here's a prayer you can pray to accept Jesus as Savior and Lord.

> Jesus, I believe you are the Son of God. Thank you that you died on the cross as a perfect sacrifice for my sins, so I can be forgiven and accepted by God. I believe you rose from the grave and have given me eternal life. I put myself in your hands as Lord of my life. Help me to follow in your footsteps, learn your ways, and live for your glory. In Jesus' name, Amen.

Contemplating His Ways:

Read chapters 6, 7, and 8 of Romans. Paul clearly presents union with Christ here. Look for the phrase "in Christ," "into Christ Jesus," "through Him," "by His life," "in God," "united together," "with Him," etc.

If you are persecuted in any way for being a Christian, Jesus is also persecuted. How can that be? How do we know that is true?

How is our God different from the gods of other religions?

CHAPTER 8

PAUL: CHRIST IN YOU AND YOU IN CHRIST

Therefore if anyone is in Christ, he is a new creation. The old has passed away. Behold, the new has come!
2 CORINTHIANS 5:17

The commission God gave me to fully proclaim to you the word of God, the mystery that was hidden for ages and generations but is now revealed to His saints....
which is Christ in you, the hope of glory.
COLOSSIANS 1:25-27

CHRIST IN YOU: A NEW CREATION

Do you have a new creation story? Maybe you just prayed the salvation prayer. That is your beginning as a new creation in Christ! My story began when I was five years old, in my bed with my mother at my side. I asked Jesus into my heart that night. It was not really dramatic, but I remember the moment and I know it changed the course of my spiritual life. Many years later, I am still discovering how my simple prayer did away with the old and called in the new. It is a lifelong and even eternal relationship that is made richer and fuller throughout our lives as we discover more and more about living united to Christ!

There are some very dramatic and unconventional new creation stories in the Bible. The thief on the cross next to Jesus, heard the malicious mockery directed at the one who had just prayed, "Father forgive them, for they don't know what they are doing." Mixed with his misery and guilt, a flame of hope rose that he also could be forgiven by this one who surely was King of the Jews, and that he could share in Jesus' kingdom to come as he shared with him in death. So, he boldly asked this King of the Jews, "Lord, remember me when You come into Your kingdom." His belief was rewarded with merciful assurance from his fellow sufferer, "Truly I tell you, today you will be with Me in Paradise" (Luke 23). The union of the Savior and the forgiven was sealed.

How was Paul joined to Jesus? When he heard the voice on the Damascus road, he immediately realized it was Jesus, and simply asked, "Lord, what do you want me to do?" He had surrendered his will to this one whom he had despised. Christ was formed in him; the new man came to life.

As Paul lay on the road, Jesus told him he would be a minister and witness to Jews and Gentiles "to open their eyes, so that they may turn from darkness to light and from the power of Satan to God, that they may receive forgiveness of sins and an inheritance among those sanctified by faith in Me.' (Acts 26:18).

By hearing and believing this very gospel message from Jesus, believers then and now are united to God. The first fourteen verses of Paul's letter to the Ephesians have been called one of the most breath-taking passages of Scripture. Paul very clearly witnesses here to what Jesus told him his message would be on the Damascus road. Paul shows us how faith in God changes our standing with him: we are "in Christ." In these verses—

> We are called the faithful *in Christ*.
> God chose us *in Christ*.

> We are blessed with every spiritual blessing *in Christ*.
> We are holy and without blame *in his presence*.
> We are adopted *in* love as sons *through Jesus Christ*.
> His grace has made us accepted *in the Beloved*.
> We have redemption, forgiveness of sin *in* Him *through his blood*.
> In the fullness of time, he will gather all things together in heaven and earth *in Christ*.
> We have obtained an inheritance *in Him*.
> We are sealed *with the Holy Spirit*.

I have italicized the important phrases that begin with the prepositions in, through, and with, that point to how we are connected to Jesus. There is a dynamic shift that happens in, through, and with new birth in Jesus in these verses. Paul expressed this shift another way a little later in his letter: "You were once darkness, but now you are light *in the Lord*. Walk as children of light" (Eph. 5:8 emphasis mine).

Paul was not a disciple who had followed Jesus for three years like Peter and John and the rest of the twelve, but he had received "an abundance of revelations" of the gospel that he preached in the years after Jesus' death and resurrection. He wrote to the Galatians, "For I would have you know, brothers, that the gospel that was preached…. I did not receive it from any man, nor was I taught it, but I received it through a revelation of Jesus Christ" (Gal. 1:11-12 ESV). How truly awesome and miraculous that the gospel Paul delivered so faithfully was revealed directly to him by Jesus in the years he spent in Damascus and Arabia after his conversion.

Today we have the privilege of learning the revelations that Jesus gave to Paul when we read the thirteen books of the Bible that he wrote. John Piper has written a tribute to Paul called, "Why I Love the Apostle Paul." Piper says, "I owe my life to the gospel of Jesus—and no one has taken me deeper into the mysteries of the gospel than Paul."[3] These mysteries are not things secret or unknown, but rather something that has been hidden in God but is now revealed. We may not fully understand things like the Trinity, the incarnation, or union, but we learn about these formerly hidden things of God in the pages of the Bible.

And no Bible author has written more about the mystery of union with Christ than Paul. Let's see where he takes us.

PAUL'S PRESENTATION OF UNION WITH CHRIST

Romans 6 through 8, written by Paul, is an especially rich passage showing us the victorious Christian life "in Christ;" in other words life in union with him. Here are verses from those chapters that show how salvation brings us into union with Jesus (emphasis mine).

> For the wages of sin is death, but the gift of God is eternal life in *Christ Jesus our Lord,* (Rom. 6:23).
> Therefore, there is now no condemnation for those who are *in Christ Jesus [in union with* the Messiah Jesus, International Standard Version] (Rom. 8:1).
> For *in Christ Jesus* the law of the Spirit of life set you free from the law of sin and death (Rom. 8:2).

Think of the great promises in just these three verses! "In Christ Jesus" we have the gift of eternal life; no condemnation; and freedom from sin and death. Paul repeats the phrase "in Christ," "in Christ Jesus," or "in Him," 164 times in his epistles according to Boice. This is a significant concept for Paul and important for us to understand! Boice says this about Paul and the doctrine, or belief in union with Christ:

> "In the writings of Paul this doctrine receives its greatest development and emphasis. In Christ alone we have

redemption, eternal life, righteousness, wisdom, freedom from the law, and every spiritual blessing."[4]

Paul shows how we share in every stage of Jesus' plan of salvation: his death, resurrection, and entrance into the glory of heaven. Here are some representative verses in Paul's writing.

We Are Crucified with Christ.
And I have been crucified with The Messiah, and from then on I myself have not been living, but The Messiah is living in me, and this that I now live in the flesh, I live by the faith of The Son of God, he who has loved us and has given himself for us (Gal. 2:20 ABPE).

We Died with Christ.
If you have died with Christ to the spiritual forces of the world, why, as though you still belonged to the world, do you submit to its regulations? (Col. 2:20).

We Were Buried with Christ.
We were therefore buried with Him through baptism into death, in order that, just as Christ was raised from the dead through the glory of the Father, we too may walk in newness of life (Rom. 6:4).

We Were Made Alive with Christ.
But God, who is rich in mercy, because of His great love with which He loved us, even when we were dead in trespasses, made us alive together with Christ (by grace you have been saved) (Eph. 2:4–5, NKJV).

We Are Presently Seated with Him in the Heavenlies.
And God raised us up with Christ and seated us with Him in the heavenly realms in Christ Jesus (Eph. 2:6).

In the next chapter we will dive deeper into what Paul has to say about our being joined to Jesus in these stages of salvation, and how our lives change in this union.

Contemplating His Ways

W. R. Newell, American Bible teacher, said, "There is scarcely a passage in the New Testament that is more delightful reading to the spiritual Christian than the eighth of Romans. . . . There is . . . a wondrous charm about the chapter. There is an atmosphere of blessing all through it." What are some specific reasons you see to explain his delight in Romans 8? What gives it the atmosphere of blessing? How do these blessings change your life?

Paul said, "I have been crucified with Christ, and I no longer live, but Christ lives *in me*" (Gal. 2:20). How do you think his life was different when he no longer lived, but Christ lived in him? How is your life different as a follower of Jesus?

CHAPTER 9

IDENTIFYING WITH JESUS IN SALVATION

And I have been crucified with The Messiah, and from then on I myself have not been living, but The Messiah is living in me.
GALATIANS 2:20 (ABPE)

Consider yourselves dead to sin and alive to God in Christ Jesus.
ROMANS 6:11

When I realized I was going home [to heaven], I felt that I was separated from my body at that very moment. I was not a body with a spirit, but a spirit surrounded by a body. I understood the truth about myself. When I said, "I'm going home," those words seemed to unlock an understanding of who I was. I questioned where those words had come from. Yet, they are words that were life to me, eternal life. They were so real that I knew that my spirit only could come to that awareness by the help of the Spirit of God who lives within my spirit, the "real" me. I just knew…that I was more connected to God than I had realized I was in the past. That connection came when I was born again, but for some reason, I wasn't aware of how strong it really was. I just knew fear was gone, and I wanted to be with my Lord and Savior forever.[5]

My friend, Dean Braxton, was pronounced clinically dead for 45 minutes in his hospital bed. He had an amazing experience going to heaven and wrote the passage above in his book, *What It Feels Like to Die*. As you can see, he is no longer in heaven; Jesus sent him back and he travels nationally and internationally delivering his powerful message about heaven and how to go there.

I was struck by him saying he knew at the moment of death that he was more connected to God than he had realized. Wouldn't it be wonderful to live every moment, realizing we are strongly connected to Jesus, our spirit with his Spirit? Dean wasn't aware how strong the connection was, but it is what took away his fear at the moment of death, and gave him the longing to be with Jesus forever. In fact, he shares that he wept when Jesus told him he needed to return to earth.

Most likely, none of you have died like Dean, but the Bible says that as a follower of Jesus, your old self has died, and it is Christ who lives in you. Another perspective from Paul is, "Consider yourselves dead to sin and alive to God in Christ Jesus." It could very well be true that like Dean, you and I don't realize the strong connection we have to God. In the Bible, this spiritual connection is compared to the union of stones in a building, branches connected to a vine, members in a human body, marriage, and even to the relationship between God the Father, the Son, and the Holy Spirit. We also see this connection in every stage of our salvation and beyond. Now, let's dive deeper into what the Bible, primarily Paul, says about the union we have with Christ in our salvation and into eternity.

UNITED WITH JESUS IN HIS DEATH

We all could list things that would make us better if they were not part of our actions or character. One way to think about those things is that they were never anything that Jesus would do or feel; they are sins against him. This sin is why we need to be "crucified with Christ." In our

IDENTIFYING WITH JESUS IN SALVATION

old nature we were living a living death leading to eternal death. "Once you were dead because of your disobedience and your many sins. You used to live in sin, just like the rest of the world, obeying the devil—the commander of the powers in the unseen world. He is the spirit at work in the hearts of those who refuse to obey God" (Eph. 2:1–2 NLT).

From God's perspective, that sinful nature must die in us, which is why he gave his Son to take all the disobedience, passionate desires, and sinful nature upon himself on the cross so we could be freed from the bondage to sin. Paul assumes such a close joining of Jesus to believers, that he says when Christ defeated sin and death by rising from the dead, we too should consider ourselves triumphant over sin and death. Because Jesus died to sin, he lives to God; we also are "alive to God [in unbroken fellowship with Him] in Christ Jesus" (Rom. 6:11 AMP).

Isaiah wrote this prophecy of Messiah's death.

> He was pierced for our transgressions,
> He was crushed for our iniquities;
> the punishment that brought us peace was upon Him,
> and by His stripes we are healed (Is. 53:5).

In a blessed exchange, Jesus bore our deserved punishment. His piercing and stripes became our peace and our healing as if we had borne the punishment; but instead, our sin was transferred to him.

There is a huge spiritual change when Jesus takes our sin upon himself. We can say, "I have been crucified with Christ, and I no longer live, but Christ lives in me" (Gal. 2:20). "My interest in the world has been crucified, and the world's interest in me has also died" (Gal. 6:14 NLT).

UNITED WITH JESUS IN BURIAL

Approaching the east bank of the Jordan River in the country of Jordan, my tour group headed to the traditional place of Jesus' baptism, called

Bethany beyond the Jordan. The flat, sandy land seemed like scorched earth with very little vegetation but was dotted with small Christian churches or ruins of ancient churches, seeming to loom up out of nowhere here and there. This was the front line in the 1967 Six-Day War and was heavily mined. It was probably a good thing I didn't know that at the time. We took a path through heavy thickets of steamy vegetation closing in on each side and overhead. Another past danger I was not aware of is described in passages in Zechariah and in Jeremiah: "Like a lion coming up from Jordan's thickets" (49:19). Maybe another good thing that I didn't know my Jeremiah that well! A colorful framed mosaic depicting Jesus standing in the Jordan with a dove on his shoulder welcomes you to the site at the river.

The Jordan River today is a small, slow-moving dirty stream; not impressive, but the site of wondrous miracles of God including Jesus' baptism. Three times God parted the water there. Joshua entered the Promised Land here with the Israelites by crossing the Jordan at flood stage. The priests stepped into the water with the ark of the covenant, and the water parted and backed up beyond sight. Elijah and Elisha walked across on dry ground just before the chariot and horses of fire took Elijah up into heaven in a whirlwind. God parted the water again for Elisha to go back to the west side. Each time, the power of God was displayed to prove his presence with individuals or the entire nation of Israel.

Think about Jesus' baptism in this river; let's look for God's message for us, even though we were not there as witnesses. John the Baptist was surprised when Jesus approached him at the Jordan and asked him to baptize him. John was baptizing those who responded to his message of repentance, so he thought that Jesus should be baptizing him instead of the other way around. Why did Jesus want John to baptize him? We can be sure he was fulfilling the will of his Father at this point, and in fact, God the Father spoke to him at his baptism. We look at Jesus' baptism as symbolic of the death he would suffer. He would be buried but rise again and enter the glory of heaven. John's baptism was a sign of burial of sin and of cleansing; when we are baptized today, it is the same sign. We are raised from deserved spiritual death so that "we serve in the new way of the Spirit, and not in the old way of the written code" (Rom. 7:6). How wonderful is it to follow in Jesus' footsteps and be raised up to serve God in a new way through his Spirit because of Jesus' sacrifice?

Jesus' baptism was a sign that he approved of John the Baptist's message of repentance and baptism. It also was a sign that Jesus was the Messiah. When Jesus came up out of the water, he saw the Spirit of God coming down like a dove on him. He heard a voice from heaven saying, "You are My beloved Son; in You I am well pleased" (Luke 3:21–22). Wouldn't you love God to say he is well pleased with you? I'm certain that God is well pleased with those who follow Jesus in baptism. Jesus was revealed as the Messiah and by baptism, we are revealed as followers of the Messiah, identifying with him in death, burial, and then resurrection.

UNITED IN JESUS' RESURRECTION

When Jesus rose from the grave, he overcame the law of sin and death. His resurrection became our resurrection. He was the perfect and final sacrifice for sin that satisfied the law of Moses. Paul shows us how we are identified with Jesus in his resurrection: "For if we have become united with Him in the likeness of His death, certainly we shall also be in the likeness of His resurrection" (Rom. 6:5); and "In Christ Jesus the law of the Spirit of life set you free from the law of sin and death" (Rom. 8:2). We will not be condemned nor be subject to eternal death when we are in Christ Jesus because he is not subject to death. We are not truly alive unless this exchange has taken place: the death of our sin for the life of Christ in us.

Let's go back to Paul's key theme of being united to Jesus. Paul said,

> Now if we died with Christ, we believe that we will also live with Him. For we know that since Christ was raised

from the dead, He cannot die again; death no longer has dominion over Him. The death He died, He died to sin once for all; but the life He lives, He lives to God. So you too must count yourselves dead to sin, but alive to God in Christ Jesus (Rom. 6:8–11).

Here again is the great exchange: dead to sin, alive to God in Christ Jesus! When we accept Jesus as Savior and Lord we are joined in union with him; because he died to sin, we also die to the dominion of sin. Jesus was freed from death and is alive to God; we also are freed from death and alive to God in Christ Jesus. This is the "newness of life" that we walk in because we are in Christ who was raised from the dead to the glory of the Father.

The same Spirit who raised Jesus from the dead is living in us and will also give life to our mortal bodies (see Rom. 8:11). Isn't it amazing that the power of the Holy Spirit that raised Jesus from the dead, is working the same power in us and will not ever allow our spirit to die? Jesus' body of flesh was set free from the law of sin and death by the Spirit of life, and we are set free by the same Spirit because we are united with him. This is our salvation. Thank you, God for this great gift!

What does it mean in practical terms to live in newness of life or to live as light in the Lord? We see some answers when we think of our life as a new creation in Christ replacing our old life that died. Our new life is the life of Christ taking over our life. The Aramaic Bible says, "And I have been crucified with The Messiah, and from then on I myself have not been living, but The Messiah is living in me" (Gal. 2:20). The life of God is given to us. This does not mean his divine nature but rather the fullness of his riches that as humans we can have when we abide in him as branches connected to the vine. God intends for his fullness to be ours. Let's look at some examples of what in his nature Jesus shares with us.

Paul prays for the Philippians, that they "may be pure and blameless for the day of Christ, filled with the fruit of righteousness that comes through Jesus Christ" (Phil. 1:10–11). Paul stresses that he has not obtained perfection, but he strives "to take hold of that for which Christ Jesus took hold of me" (Phil. 3:8–12). Like Paul, let us press on to gain the righteousness of Christ through faith. This is what Jesus offers, and why he took hold of us!

The grace, faith, and love that are in Christ Jesus is meant to overflow in our lives (1 Tim. 1:14). Anyone who abides in love abides in Christ and Christ in him. "By this, love is perfected with us, so that we may have confidence in the day of judgment; because as He is, so also are we in this world" (1 John 4:17). John simply states that as Christians we should be a living likeness of Jesus!

UNITED ETERNALLY WITH JESUS

And God raised us up with Christ and seated us with Him in the heavenly realms in Christ Jesus.
EPHESIANS 2:6

Oh how the grace flows. It is at the altar when I pray for love, and love the people, that the anointing flows!! I am in heaven.

I found this journal entry my husband, Evan, wrote after a service in Brazil where he gave the gospel message and prayed for healing. His journal is full of stories of people he prayed for who were healed. Evan is in heaven with Jesus now, but for him, it was heaven on earth to see God's love for the people he ministered to. It was heaven to be a minister of God's saving and healing glory for so many of these loved ones in Brazil and other countries.

Ephesians 2:6 above says that when we put our faith and trust in Jesus, we are seated with him in the heavenly realms. Really though, it doesn't take too long to figure out when you look around that we are not exactly situated in heaven! Let's look at how this verse fits in the context, Ephesians 2:4–7.

> But God, who is rich in mercy, because of His great love with which He loved us, even when we were dead in trespasses, made us alive *together* with Christ (by grace you have been saved), and raised us up *together*, and made us sit *together* in the heavenly places in Christ Jesus, that in the ages to come He might show the exceeding riches of His grace in His kindness toward us in Christ Jesus (NKJV emphasis mine).

This verse is not only talking about heaven when we die. Notice the word together used three times above. We are raised up from death to life together with Christ; this is God's ultimate plan because of his great love for us! Our connection to Jesus is so close that because he enters heaven, we do as well. Even on earth we can expect to share in the glory of heaven together with our Lord Christ Jesus. This is the glory that Evan felt as God used him to bless and show God's grace to so many.

In Philippians, Paul says, "I want to know Christ and the power of His resurrection" (3:10). Through that resurrection power we are raised to heavenly places when we are in him. Maclaren comments on this verse: "It is only if we are in Him that there is so real a unity of life between Him and us that there enters into us some breath of His own life."[6] The life Jesus gives us is heavenly, not earthly. In his High Priestly Prayer, John 17, Jesus prays to his Father at the end of the Passover feast before going out to the Garden of Gethsemane. He prays on behalf of his disciples with him that evening:

> I am not asking that You take them out of the world, but that You keep them from the evil one. They are not of the world, as I am not of the world (John 17:15–16).

IDENTIFYING WITH JESUS IN SALVATION

Jesus' followers are in the world, but they are not "of the world" because they are in Christ, and he is not of the world.

Paul tells the Ephesians that in Christ and through faith in him, we can enter God's presence with boldness and confidence (Eph. 3:12). Remember Jesus taught us to pray to our Father in heaven? Then Paul demonstrates that boldness by praying the following prayer to God. Does this sound heavenly or earthly?

> I ask that out of the riches of His glory He may strengthen you with power through His Spirit in your inner being, so that Christ may dwell in your hearts through faith. Then you, being rooted and grounded in love, will have power, together with all the saints, to comprehend the length and width and height and depth of the love of Christ, and to know this love that surpasses knowledge, that you may be filled with all the fullness of God.
>
> Now to Him who is able to do immeasurably more than all we ask or imagine, according to His power that is at work within us, to Him be the glory in the church and in Christ Jesus throughout all generations, forever and ever. Amen" (Eph. 3:16–21).

This great soaring prayer could only be describing what it must be like dwelling "not of the world," but in heavenly places with Christ. The wonderful thing is that this prayer is for those who have Christ's power at work in them here and now, not just in heaven. This is a prayer that Paul prays with confidence that God will hear and answer. The answers place us in heavenly places while in this earthly body.

This prayer asks for grace and blessing that could only come from heavenly places. The love, power, glory, and strength that Paul prays for are ours in this life when we are in Christ. We are raised up to this reality with Christ and are seated with him in the heavenly realms with love, power, glory and strength in Christ Jesus.

And finally, this heavenly power will raise the servants of Christ from the grave because we are in him. This is how we will share in Jesus' final triumph over death. And in him we share the glories of heaven both now and in eternity. This is glorious, amazing grace!

SUMMARY

In Romans 6, Paul gives us a powerful summary of how our salvation identifies with Jesus in his death, burial, and resurrection. We will visit some of the additional themes later.

> Have you forgotten that when we were joined with Christ Jesus in baptism, we joined him in his death? For we died and were buried with Christ by baptism. And just as Christ was raised from the dead by the glorious power of the Father, now we also may live new lives.
>
> Since we have been united with him in his death, we will also be raised to life as he was. We know that our old sinful selves were crucified with Christ so that sin might lose its power in our lives. We are no longer slaves to sin. For when we died with Christ we were set free from the power of sin. And since we died with Christ, we know we will also live with him. We are sure of this because Christ was raised from the dead, and he will never die again. Death no longer has any power over him. When he died, he died once to break the power of sin. But now that he lives, he lives for the glory of God. So you also should consider yourselves to be dead to the power of sin and alive to God through Christ Jesus.
>
> Do not let sin control the way you live; do not give in to sinful desires. Do not let any part of your body become

an instrument of evil to serve sin. Instead, give yourselves completely to God, for you were dead, but now you have new life. So use your whole body as an instrument to do what is right for the glory of God. Sin is no longer your master, for you no longer live under the requirements of the law. Instead, you live under the freedom of God's grace (Rom. 6:3–14 NLT).

Contemplating His Ways

Do you think of going to heaven as "I'm going home?" Dean said he didn't realize how strong his connection to God was. How strong is your connection? Is it strong enough to overcome fear of death?

What are some actions you do or attitudes you have that Jesus would not do or have?

Paul said, "So you also should consider yourselves to be dead to the power of sin and alive to God through Christ Jesus" (Rom. 6:8–11). Why did he say that? How do you do that?

CHAPTER 10

JESUS TEACHES SOMETHING NEW

*"Unless you are born again,
you can't be part of the kingdom of God."—Jesus*
JOHN 3:3

*"Anyone who lives by the truth comes to the light, so that his
works may be shown to be accomplished by God."—Jesus*
JOHN 3:21

We all enjoy new things. Maybe it's a new recipe, a new watch, a new car, a new tool, a new book, etc. But most of us would agree a new baby in the family is the best of all! I remember standing by my first baby's crib, watching every little move on her face or hands as she slept. Then years later, I was enthralled with her own baby, my first grandchild! What a wonder new life is! No wonder Jesus spoke of new life in him as being born again; it is the beginning of an entirely new family relationship based on love, with the God of the universe.

We have looked at new creation stories that tell how different ones were born again into the kingdom of God. Even Old Testament prophets foretold something new was coming. Isaiah hinted at the glories of a coming Savior and a changing relationship with God. A "new thing" was an important theme for Isaiah (emphasis mine).

> "Do not call to mind the former things; pay no attention to the things of old. Behold, I am about to do *something new*; even now it is coming. Do you not see it? Indeed, I will make a way in the wilderness and streams in the desert" (Is. 43:18–19).
> "From now on I will tell you of *new things*, hidden things unknown to you." (Is. 48:6).
> "Behold, the former things have happened, and now I declare *new things*. Before they spring forth I proclaim them to you" (Is. 42:9).

And Isaiah gives a glimpse ahead at what the new thing was!

> And in that day it will be said, "Surely this is our God; we have waited for Him, and He has saved us. This is the Lord for whom we have waited. Let us rejoice and be glad in His salvation" (Is. 25:9).

Even though the Jews of Jesus' day were very well versed in these prophecies, when Jesus came, many were not prepared to accept him and his message of being born again as a new creation formed by God.

Nicodemus certainly found it hard to understand the revolutionary statement Jesus made the night he came to him, "Listen. I'm telling you the truth. Unless you are born again, you can't be part of the kingdom of God" (John 3:3, my paraphrase).

"How can a man be born when he is old? He cannot enter a second time into his mother's womb and be born, can he?" Nicodemus asked bluntly, thinking it was an outlandish thing Jesus was saying. But just think, if we were not familiar with this phrase, "born again," we would have no idea what Jesus was talking about either!

Jesus answered him, "Do not be amazed that I said to you, 'You must be born again.' The wind blows where it wishes, and you hear the sound of it, but you do not know where it is coming from and where it is going; so is everyone who has been born of the Spirit" (See John 3:4–20 NASB).

Jesus tells Nicodemus that he must be born of the Spirit, who is the source of holiness of the heart. Being born again brings an end to the first birth, which Paul calls the "old man" and ushers in a new creation in the Holy Spirit who forms a new nature, new values, and new purpose. What could symbolize a greater change of state and character than newly born life? The old life is gone, replaced by the new, a gift from heaven and not something anyone could do for themselves.

Jesus continued talking to Nicodemus and spoke about himself in words that may be the most familiar in the whole Bible. He said, "For God loved the world in this way: He gave his one and only Son, so that everyone who believes in him will not perish but have eternal life. . . . Anyone who believes in him is not condemned, but anyone who does not believe is already condemned, because he has not believed in the name of the one and only Son of God. . . . But anyone who lives by the truth comes to the light, so that his works may be shown to be accomplished by God" (John 3:16, 18, 21, CSB). Living by the truth can only be done with a life in union with Christ Jesus. Only when Jesus is living in us, and not our old self, will our works represent God's work in us. Only when his life is lived through our lives does God receive the glory and honor for the good that we do. When Jesus comes in his glory, he will reveal what he has accomplished through us (Matt. 25:31–46).

It is probable that Nicodemus decided he wanted to live by the truth and come to the light, so that his works would be "accomplished by God." The Bible includes the account of how Nicodemus helped Joseph of Arimathea prepare Jesus' body for burial, bringing many pounds of costly spices to anoint his body (John 19:39). An honorable burial for his Son was a work accomplished by God through Joseph and Nicodemus.

Because being born again was a spiritual reality and like the wind impossible to see, it was hard for Nicodemus to believe. But this was Jesus' message to Nicodemus and to us! John wrote, "If you know that He is righteous, you know that everyone who practices righteousness is born of Him" (1 John 2:29 NKJV). Paul described this new birth through Jesus Christ, saying, "Therefore if anyone is in Christ, he is a new creation. The old has passed away. Behold, the new has come!" (2 Cor. 5:17). Everyone who believes in Jesus experiences a new birth into the kingdom of God, and enters into eternal life. The life that Jesus gives is his own and it is eternal. Peter wrote, "Blessed be the God and Father of our Lord Jesus Christ! By His great mercy He has given us new birth into a living hope" (1 Peter 1:3). Being born into the family of God comes with the living hope of eternal relationship with him.

Jesus began preaching this gospel of a living hope first in Galilee, saying, "The time is fulfilled . . . and the kingdom of God is near. Repent and believe in the gospel!" (Mark 1:15). The Pharisees asked him when the kingdom of God would come. Jesus made it clear that the kingdom would not make a visible entrance like a king arriving with great pomp, but rather he told them, "The kingdom of God is within you" (Luke 17:21 NKJV). Jesus wanted them to know his reign would be in the heart of those joined to him, not a physical force to overcome any earthly kingdom, which is what they expected. Paul later wrote in Romans, "The kingdom of God is not a matter of eating and drinking, but of righteousness, peace, and joy in the Holy Spirit" (14:17). What blessings the kingdom of God brings to our hearts: righteousness, peace, and joy in the Holy Spirit!

When we read in Matthew how Jesus sent out his twelve disciples, we see how he considered them joined to him. He gave them his power to cast out demons and to heal all kinds of diseases. He told them to preach, "The kingdom of heaven is at hand." He told them to heal the sick, raise the dead, and cast out demons. They would do this because they had freely received the power of Jesus so they could freely manifest the life, healing, and deliverance that came from Jesus (Matt. 10:1, 7–8).

In his further instructions to the twelve, he told them they would be brought before governors and kings as witnesses, but "do not worry about how to respond or what to say. In that hour you will be given what to say. For it will not be you speaking, but the Spirit of your Father speaking through you" (Matt. 10:19-20). Can you imagine how comforting that was for the disciples to know the Spirit of God would speak through them? What confidence that inspires! Because we are united with him, we can have that confidence as well. The Spirit of God lives in us!

Even though Jesus reassured his disciples that the Holy Spirit would speak through them, he warned them of the additional challenges and tribulation they would face:

> You will be hated by everyone because of My name, but the one who perseveres to the end will be saved. . . . A disciple is not above his teacher, nor a servant above his master. It is enough for a disciple to be like his teacher, and a servant like his master. If the head of the house has been called Beelzebul, how much more the members of his household! (Matt. 10:22, 24-25).

The wonderful thing here is that Jesus calls the twelve disciples members of his household. Their goal is to become like him, their teacher and master; but because of their connection to him, they would be hated as his disciples. Circumstances would not be easier for them than for their teacher. What they could hope for was to be like him and serve him as master and teacher.

Jesus was called Beelzebul, related to an especially insulting name for Satan; as his disciples, they could expect to be called that and even more disgusting names. Jesus did not promise ease for them. As followers of Jesus, we should not expect it. But what a wonder to be called members of his family, to serve him and learn from him, to bear his name and bear his likeness!

Contemplating His Ways

Do you think God gives power today to heal the sick, raise the dead, and cast out demons as he gave to his twelve disciples? Why or why not?

John 3:21 says, "But anyone who lives by the truth comes to the light, so that his works may be shown to be accomplished by God." Can others say your works are accomplished by God? What has God accomplished by being in union with you?

In Matthew 10 above, Jesus showed his disciples their goal was to be like him, their teacher and master. Is this your goal as a disciple of Jesus? How do we learn from Jesus, our teacher and master, today?

CHAPTER 11

JESUS TEACHES ON UNION WITH HIM

*"Truly, truly, I tell you, whoever receives the one
I send receives Me, and whoever receives Me
receives the One who sent Me."*
JOHN 13:20

THAT YOU DO NOT FALL AWAY

If you opened your Bible to the first verse of John 16 and read what Jesus said, "I have told you these things so that you will not fall away," you probably would want to go back and read what "these things" were in the previous chapter or chapters, in this case Chapters 14 and 15. It turns out Jesus was in the middle of speaking to his eleven disciples at Passover, the night of his betrayal and arrest. His words that night take on the importance of parting words; these will be words he knows his disciples will need in the coming hours in order to strengthen their faith. For this reason, they are important words for us as well. We need to hear those things so that we also do not fall away.

Judas had already left that night, realizing this would be a good opportunity to hand Jesus over to the chief priests. Before he left, however, Jesus shared the Passover meal with him and had washed his feet, all the while knowing he would betray him. In this longest recorded speech of Jesus, he will reveal how united he is to his disciples. Let's take a look.

John gives a detailed account of Jesus' words to his disciples in these last few hours together. This Upper Room Discourse, chapters 13 to 17 of John, is ultimately a wonderful look into how Jesus loved and comforted his disciples even while letting them know what would soon happen. No wonder the disciples needed consolation and questions answered that night. He told them he was going away, and they could not follow him until later. Perhaps most comforting to them was when Jesus told them they would be joined to him as branches joined to the vine and that he would send the Holy Spirit, the Helper who would testify of him after he was gone.

Can you imagine the emotions Jesus was feeling in those last hours with the faithful ones who had followed him for three years? I believe above all it was great love for them and his desire to show them how much he loved them. John introduces his story of that Last Supper this way: "It was now just before the Passover Feast, and Jesus knew that His hour had come to leave this world and return to the Father. Having loved His own who were in the world, He loved them to the very end."

The act of washing the disciples' feet was the first of many expressions of Jesus' love for them that night. As their Lord and Teacher, he washed their feet. "I have set you an example so that you should do as I have done for you" (13:15); they should wash one another's feet. He had openly shown humility and how he loved them. They, and we, should want to do the same, loving and serving with humility.

Jesus had spoken earlier to the disciples of his death and even his resurrection, but on this night, it is coming soon. This is what he says:

> Little children, I am with you only a little while longer. You will look for Me, and as I said to the Jews, so now I say to you: "Where I am going, you cannot come." A new commandment I give you: Love one another. As I have

loved you, so you also must love one another. By this everyone will know that you are My disciples, if you love one another (John 13:33–35).

Jesus knew how important it was for his "little children" to love each other through the hard times ahead: his death, departure, and the persecution of those who would later be called Christians. Their love for each other would be so unique and evident that it would be a sign to everyone that they are disciples of Jesus Christ, loving as he loved.

It was not an easy thing he asked: love each other as I have loved you. Jesus tells them, "If anyone loves Me, he will keep My word. My Father will love him, and We will come to him and make Our home with him" (14:23). This is how they can love as Jesus loved. Not only will Jesus make his home with them giving them power to love like him and to do his will, but his Father will make his home with them as well! The union of the Father and Son is one of the illustrations Jesus gave to the disciples to help them understand his similar union with them. At the Last Supper, he wanted to comfort and prepare them for his departure so he told them how closely he was connected to them and would be in the future, taking them from what they already knew about common relationships to what he wanted them to learn about his union with them. They knew how fathers relate to their children; Jesus uses his own relationship of oneness with his Father to show them he wants union with them as well.

We do not understand the mystery of the Trinity, the oneness of the Father, Son, and Holy Spirit, and our union with the Lord Jesus is not on that level. Theirs is a union of equality in essence and nature, as divine, eternal beings. As created beings, we will never be divine, but we understand the father to son relationship that Jesus uses for comparison. The union of the Son to God the Father, and also Jesus' union with believers are unions of life and love.

Jesus speaks multiple times in these last hours with the disciples, about his oneness with the Father and how this oneness is mirrored in his relationship with his followers. He refers to his Father fifty-seven times in chapters thirteen to sixteen of John, and then the entire seventeenth chapter is his prayer to the Father. Let's consider ourselves part of the group that Jesus is speaking to in the upper room. He reveals that in a little while the world will not see him anymore, "But you will see Me. Because I live, you also will live. On that day you will know that I am in My Father, and you are in Me, and I am in you" (John 14:19–20). Jesus would return to heaven. The disciples would not see him after that, and we do not see Jesus in the world today, but like the disciples, we see Jesus because we are in him, and he is in us.

Moreover, when Jesus said we will live because he lives, we know that we have the eternal life of Jesus. When we love Jesus by keeping his commandments, we are loved by the Father and by Jesus who will reveal himself to us. Remember, they will come and make their home with us. Take comfort! Let not your heart be troubled.

At one point in the Passover meal, Philip asked Jesus to show them the Father. Jesus answers him that as he listened to and observed Jesus, he was listening to and observing the Father. "Do you not believe that I am in the Father and the Father is in Me? The words I say to you, I do not speak on My own. Instead, it is the Father dwelling in Me, performing His works (John 14:10). Jesus did not speak or act on his own. The Father spoke and acted through him. This is our goal, speaking and acting as Jesus directs, not on our own.

He adds a promise that draws us into the equation: "Whoever believes in me will also do the works that I do, and even greater works" (John 14:12 my paraphrase). This is the concept behind Jesus saying, "And whatever you might ask in My name, this I will do, so that the Father may be glorified in the Son" (14:13). Jesus promises to do what believers in him ask so that the works he did are multiplied in them throughout the earth and throughout the ages. It is amazing that Jesus brings glory to God the Father by answering our prayers!

THAT YOUR JOY MAY BE COMPLETE

Remember Jesus told his disciples that he was telling them things that would keep them from falling away when he was no longer on earth. Let's turn our attention to another "I have told you these things" passage. In John 15:11, Jesus says, "I have told you these things so that My joy may be in you and your joy may be complete." This is going to be good! What did Jesus say previous to this that would give complete joy to those in the room that night? Let's listen too because we are included as his children.

Jesus showed how closely he would be joined to his disciples even after his departure by making a key comparison of his relationship with them to how a vine and its branches are connected. As branches live and bear fruit only when they are joined to the vine, so his followers receive life and bear fruit only in intimate connection to Jesus. Jesus intended for that to bring them and us complete joy! Notice how many times Jesus uses "abide" in this passage!

> I am the vine, you are the branches. He who *abides* in Me, and I in him, bears much fruit; for without Me you can do nothing. If anyone does not *abide* in Me, he is cast out as a branch and is withered; and they gather them and throw them into the fire, and they are burned. If you *abide* in Me, and My words *abide* in you, you will ask what you desire, and it shall be done for you. By this My Father is glorified, that you bear much fruit; so you will be My disciples. As the Father loved Me, I also have loved you; *abide* in My love. If you keep My commandments, you will *abide* in My love, just as I have kept My Father's commandments and *abide* in His love (John 15:5–10, NKJV, emphasis mine).

Abiding (remaining, staying, dwelling) in the love of Jesus is what would give them the joy of Jesus, which is complete joy. There is nothing Jesus desired more than that his beloved ones abide in his love, which flows from him as life from a vine. And now we know what it was that Jesus intended to bring joy to those listening that night.

Did you notice Jesus didn't just say, "You will have joy?" He said, "my joy" will be in you, and will be complete. We can have the joy of Jesus, just as we have his love coming into our branch from his vine. Our joy can only be complete when we have the joy of Jesus. That is what he offers to us as his disciples.

Who cannot relate to Jesus' teaching here, and understand the life-giving connection between the vine and the branches as a parallel of the union between him and us as individual believers? All the nourishment of each branch passes first through the main vine that springs from the earth. In the same way, Jesus is the source of all life, grace, mercy, love, wisdom, joy, and strength that comes to us. He is our leader and teacher imparting all we need to bear fruits of holiness. This is how God could say, "be holy as I am holy" (Lev. 11:44) or "love one another as I have loved you" (John 15:12).

LOVE FROM THE VINE

We can follow the thread of John's thoughts about abiding in God as it relates to a favorite theme of his, which is love. In 1 John 4:16–17 he writes:

> We have come to know and have believed the love which God has for us. God is love, and the one who abides in love abides in God, and God abides in him. By this, love is perfected with us.

The love of God streams from the vine into the branches when they remain attached to the vine. To abide in love is to abide in God, and God in us.

Here is the rest of the joy-filled story. The disciples knew Jesus wanted them to have his joy as he abides in them, and as they abide in him. His resurrection three days later brought them great joy as well as assurance of his unceasing love for them. In his last words before he was carried up into heaven, he promised the coming of the Holy Spirit, and blessed them. No wonder they worshiped him and returned to Jerusalem "with great joy."

In the next chapter we will look into this promise of the Holy Spirit and how his presence in our lives assures us that we are connected to the vine!

Contemplating His Ways

Jesus asked the twelve to love one another the way he loved them. How did Jesus love them? How does he love us? How do we know when we are loving like him?

How as a branch, do you stay connected to the vine of the life of Jesus? How does that bring joy into your life?

Do you sometimes feel abandoned by God? What did Jesus say to his disciples at Passover that could be a message for you?

CHAPTER 12

UNION BY THE HOLY SPIRIT

By this we know that we abide in Him, and He in us, because He has given us of His Spirit.
1 JOHN 4:13 NKJV

Those controlled by the flesh cannot please God. You, however, are controlled not by the flesh, but by the Spirit, if the Spirit of God lives in you. And if anyone does not have the Spirit of Christ, he does not belong to Christ.
ROMANS 8:8–9

I sat in the front row at Evan's memorial service, surrounded by those who came to show their love, respect, and support. I had been so blessed earlier, greeting many family members, friends, and neighbors. Now, it was as if I were floating on the love I felt, and a warm blanket had settled on my shoulders, comforting and protecting me. This was a new, unexpected feeling, but I knew it was the comfort of the Holy Spirit, holding me up, carrying me as we paid tribute to Evan's life, especially to how his connection to the Lord Jesus shaped his life and how he had been a blessing to others. In the following days, it was the Holy Spirit who spoke comfort through the Scriptures, assuring me that Evan had entered the heavenly places and was now eternally with Jesus and loved ones who had gone before, waiting for me and the rest of his family to join him there.

I was not abandoned, just as Jesus' followers were not abandoned when he left the earth. None of us is left alone even in the loneliest, darkest times in our lives. Essentially, it is through the gift and promise of the Holy Spirit that our union with Jesus is accomplished. Through the Holy Spirit, the fountain of the life of Jesus has come to abide in our hearts, assuring us of God's presence and protection. C. S. Lewis wrote, "The principal reason underlying all the other magnificent reasons that God the Son united himself to our humanity is this: that by the Holy Spirit we may be united to Christ and so enjoy his fellowship with the Father forever."[7]

Jesus told us how this will happen. Let's look in again as he speaks at that last Passover.

> "I will ask the Father, and He will give you another Helper [Comforter, Advocate, Intercessor—Counselor, Strengthener, Standby AMP], that He may be with you forever; that is the Spirit of truth, whom the world cannot receive, because it does not see Him or know Him, but you know Him because He abides with you and will be in you. I will not leave you as orphans; I will come to you" (John 14:16–18 NASB 1995).

This was the comforting word the disciples needed to hear. Jesus was leaving but would not leave them as children with no father! This message is for us too! The Father has sent the Spirit of truth to us. We are not orphans. Jesus said, "I will come to you." We are reminded with these sweet words that we are his children, and that it is Jesus who has come to us in the form of the Holy Spirit, demonstrating his and our union with the Holy Spirit who will dwell in each individual believer. As a parent would not leave his child, Jesus will always be united with us by the presence of his Holy Spirit. He has come to us!

UNION BY THE HOLY SPIRIT

As part of God's family, the disciples would not be abandoned. They would continue to be his disciples and Jesus would be their Lord and Teacher through the presence of the Holy Spirit. The only way they would be able to love like Jesus, keep his commandments, and do his works would be in union with him through his indwelling Spirit who would be given to them. They would be eternally united to Jesus in the Spirit. This is why Jesus could say, "Let not your heart be troubled," that he would never leave nor forsake them, and that his complete joy would be in them as well. Can you accept this as your own message from Jesus?

ARRIVAL OF THE HOLY SPIRIT

Jesus chose Peter to be a leader in the early church. The third time Jesus appeared to the disciples after his resurrection, he prepared breakfast for them on the shore of the Sea of Galilee while they were out fishing. When Peter realized it was the Lord calling to them, he plunged into the sea and swam to Jesus. You have to smile at this bold, eager man who loved his resurrected Lord, even after the shame of denying him three times as Jesus said he would. When they finished breakfast that morning, Jesus asked Peter three times, "Do you love me?" Then three times Jesus set before him a ministry that Peter could not have understood at that time: "Feed my lambs;" "Tend my sheep;" and "Feed my sheep" (John 21). After all, he was a fisherman!

Just days after Jesus ascended into heaven, this man, who had denied Jesus because he was so frightened to be associated with him, was standing up and preaching the gospel of Jesus to a huge crowd who were in Jerusalem for the festival of Shavuot, called Pentecost in the New Testament. What happened that turned Peter from a denier into a powerful preacher who was "feeding the sheep?"

During the festival, the Holy Spirit had fallen on all the followers of Jesus who had assembled together in a house. There was a sound from heaven like a rushing mighty wind and fire-like tongues sat on each one. The sound was so loud, a great crowd gathered. They all heard "the wonderful works of God" in their own language as those who were anointed spoke.

This was Peter's opportunity to preach about Jesus to the huge crowd. No longer the frightened denier, he finished with this challenge: "Repent and be baptized, every one of you, in the name of Jesus Christ for the forgiveness of your sins, and you will receive the gift of the Holy Spirit. This promise belongs to you and your children and to all who are far off" (Acts 2). We know the Holy Spirit fell on many that day because they were "cut to the heart;" three thousand souls were added to the young church. What a thrill to know this promise of the Holy Spirit that Peter spoke of belongs to us who are called by God today!

It's important to understand who the Holy Spirit is, the gift and the promise Peter preached about at Pentecost. Peter illustrated the work of each, Father, Son, and Holy Spirit in his gospel sermon: repent and be baptized in the name of Jesus whose sacrifice provided forgiveness of sins, and receive the gift of the Holy Spirit whom the Lord our God has promised. Jesus has come to us in the person of the Holy Spirit, sent by God. God is real! The disciples experienced this at Pentecost and we can too! R. T. Kendall writes, "The person of Jesus was as real to [the disciples] by the Spirit as He had been previously to them when they saw Him in the flesh.[8] This is the Advantage that we have! The Holy Spirit was then and is today applying the redemption of Jesus to the hearts of people. Jesus has come, dwelling in union by the Spirit within those whom God has called.

Contemplating His Ways

C. S. Lewis said the principal reason Jesus came to earth was so the Holy Spirit could unite us to him, and so enjoy the fellowship he had with the Father forever. Why did he believe that? How do we enjoy fellowship with the Father? Use I John 1:3 for reference.

The coming of the Holy Spirit was a pivotal event in Peter's life. Have you experienced a similar event in your life? How did it change you?

CHAPTER 13

THE ADVANTAGE OF THE HOLY SPIRIT

"But I tell you the truth, it is to your advantage that I go away; for if I do not go away, the Helper will not come to you; but if I go, I will send Him to you"
JOHN 16:7 NASB 1995

Hold on to the pattern of sound teaching you have heard me, with the faith and love that are in Christ Jesus. Guard the treasure entrusted to you, with the help of the Holy Spirit who dwells in us.
2 TIMOTHY 1:13–14

The promise of the Holy Spirit endures from Old Testament times until the present. Beginning with Old Testament prophecies, we'll take a look at the role the Holy Spirit played in Jesus' ministry, as well as his role in believers' lives today. We will see that God ministered to Jesus on earth through the Holy Spirit in many of the same ways that he does to us today through the same Holy Spirit.

ISAIAH'S PROPHECY

In Nazareth, there is a property that has been designed to look like a village in Jesus' day, with people (as well as animals!) playing the role of residents. Crops like those that would have been grown in Jesus' day flourish on a steep, terraced hill that today is overlooked by high-rise apartments at the top. Our guide took us to an olive tree that had small shoots bravely rising from the stump. He reminded our group of the prophecy in Isaiah about the Messiah:

> There shall come forth a shoot from the stump of Jesse, and a branch from his roots shall bear fruit. And the Spirit of the LORD shall rest upon him, the Spirit of wisdom and understanding, the Spirit of counsel and might, the Spirit of knowledge and the fear of the LORD (Is. 11:1–2 ESV).

This prophecy was fulfilled in Jesus. Isaiah foresaw his coming and declared the Spirit of *Yahweh*, usually translated *Lord*, would rest on Jesus and would be the Spirit of wisdom and understanding, counsel and might, and knowledge and the fear of the Lord. There would be no barriers between Jesus and his Father who chose to anoint him with these qualities, which he needed and used to the fullest extent in his time on earth. Jesus chose to humble himself, becoming in appearance as a man, obedient to the point of death on the cross (Phil. 2:8). In his humility, he was in subjection to his Father and the Holy Spirit. Let's look at Isaiah's prophecy about the characteristics of the Spirit of the Lord that rested on Jesus. The possibilities for us to live under the influence of the same Spirit are revealed here as much as his influence on Jesus' character. The same Spirit that the Father gave to Jesus, he has given to us!

The Spirit of the Lord

> "The Spirit of the Lord is on Me, because He has anointed Me

> *to preach good news to the poor. He has sent Me to proclaim*
> *liberty to the captives and recovery of sight to the blind,*
> *to release the oppressed,"*
> LUKE 4:18

Jesus understood the role of the Holy Spirit who was his own personal companion in life on earth. He was present beginning at his conception, during his childhood, and when God visibly anointed him with his Spirit in the form of a dove at his baptism. The Spirit of *Yahweh* was not just a dove that rested on Jesus temporarily. The coming of the Holy Spirit in a visible form was a sign to all that Jesus Christ was anointed by God as the Messiah and was united to the Father through his Holy Spirit, ready to fulfill God's will on earth. "For in Christ all the fullness of the Deity dwells in bodily form" (Col. 2:9). Fully God, but also fully man, Jesus would be equipped to speak the Word of God on earth through union with the Father and the Holy Spirit.

Jesus had limitless God-given attributes through the Spirit. In his commentary on Isaiah 11, MacLaren says, "There has never been but one manhood capable of receiving and retaining the whole fullness of the Spirit of God."[9] Jesus came, lived a perfect life, and offered himself a sacrifice to God to save those who believe in him from eternal death. The Holy Spirit that was given to Jesus ministered not only to him, but to all those who even today choose to unite with him. "For from His fullness, we have all received and grace upon grace" (John 1:16).

Jesus knew from experience the importance of the Spirit's work, which is why he said to his disciples at Passover, "But I tell you the truth, it is to your advantage that I go away; for if I do not go away, the Helper will not come to you; but if I go, I will send Him to you" (John 16:7 NASB 1995). He wanted them to have the ministry of the Holy Spirit who had helped him to remain pure in his human nature even though he was tempted in every way just as they would be and as we are (Heb. 4:15); he wanted them to abide in love and obedience to the will of God throughout the many challenges he knew they would experience. John later reminded

Christians in the churches he oversaw, that they had Jesus Christ as advocate through the Holy Spirit; "My little children, I am writing these things to you so that you will not sin. But if anyone does sin, we have an advocate before the Father—Jesus Christ, the Righteous One" (1John 2:1).

Jesus is still sending the Helper. Through the Holy Spirit Christ now dwells in believers, uniting them to himself, and to each other as the body of Christ. What Jesus is, he gives to his followers so that they can live his likeness through the same Spirit of the Lord that rested on him. "He who unites himself with the Lord is one with Him in spirit" (1 Cor. 6:17). Jesus shows us the possibility and the beauty of a holy life, even in our human flesh. Paul said, "Those controlled by the flesh cannot please God. You, however, are controlled not by the flesh, but by the Spirit, if the Spirit of God lives in you" (Rom. 8:8–9).

The Spirit of Wisdom and Understanding

> *This also comes from the LORD of Hosts, who is wonderful in counsel and excellent in wisdom.*
> ISAIAH 28:29

> *In Him we have redemption through His blood, the forgiveness of our trespasses, according to the riches of His grace that He lavished on us with all wisdom and understanding.*
> EPHESIANS 1:7–8

The verse in Isaiah above puzzled me. Why was it the summary of a passage about planting black cumin, wheat, barley and spelt? I read it over and over trying to figure out the connections between planting crops and the wonderful counsel and excellent wisdom of God. To give you the context, at the time I was battling cancer, diagnosed a year after Evan's death. I believe the Holy Spirit led me to research black cumin which is mentioned five times in two verses. I found a connection! The National

Library of Medicine reported, "*Nigella sativa* [black cumin] has been used as traditional medicine for centuries. . . . The anti-cancer activities of *N. sativa* components were recognized thousands of years ago but proper scientific research with this important traditional medicine is a very recent story." This was a discovery for me but not surprising considering the excellent wisdom of God who created plants that man would need for both food and medicine. I believe God gave me this understanding to set me on a path to look for natural healing methods. I am so thankful to God that I am cancer-free today!

Isaiah said the Spirit of wisdom and the Spirit of understanding would rest upon Jesus. The Bible has much to say about wisdom. In fact, Job, Psalms, Proverbs, Ecclesiastes, and the Song of Solomon are usually grouped together as Wisdom Writings. Other countries of the ancient Near East beside Israel had schools of wisdom. Egypt has written proverbs and sayings from as early as 2700 B.C., which are similar in style to the wisdom literature of Israel. However, only in the Hebrew culture was the one righteous God given credit as the source of wisdom. We see this righteous standard from the beginning of Proverbs. Solomon writes in his introduction "The fear of the Lord is the beginning of knowledge, but fools despise wisdom and discipline [instruction NKJV]" (Prov. 1:7).

Wisdom is personified in the book of Proverbs as a woman who cries out in the public places of the city, and who in other places gives instruction to a youth as in this passage.

> My son, if you accept my words and hide my commandments within you, so that you incline your ear to wisdom and direct your heart to understanding … if you seek it like silver and search it out like hidden treasure; then you will discern the fear of the Lord and discover the knowledge of God. For the Lord gives wisdom; from His mouth come knowledge and understanding" (Prov. 2:1-2, 4-6).

Jesus, like many Hebrew youth, would most likely have memorized these verses about the Spirit of wisdom, along with many other Spirit-breathed Old Testament passages. Jesus' delight was in the Law of the Lord, meditating on it day and night. Many times, as he spoke to crowds, he relied on the Spirit of wisdom and understanding by using Old Testament Scriptures, signaled by saying, "It is written. . . . " When he taught the people in his hometown, they were astonished. "Where did this man get such wisdom and miraculous powers?" they asked (Matt. 13:54).

There is a site often visited by tourists in Israel where Peter made the revolutionary statement, "You are the Messiah, the Son of the living God" (Matt. 16:16 CSB) Twenty-five miles north of the Sea of Galilee, Caesarea Philippi in the foothills of Mount Herman, was the farthest north that Jesus walked in Israel. From ancient times it had been a hotbed of pagan worship of Baal, and in Jesus' day, the Greek god Pan was worshiped there; for this reason, few pious Jews ever went there. Large Greek and Roman temples had been built backing up to a high red rock cliff where a gushing spring came out of a gaping, deep hole in the cliff. The people had long believed this was the "gate of hell" and human sacrifices were made there to the gods. Today ruins of these temples remain, but perhaps most enduring are the many niches carved into the face of the cliff, where statues of Pan would have been placed. Why would Jesus have taken several days of rough travel to go there with his disciples? It is certain that he had a reason to bring his followers to this place. The record of the conversation there gives some clues.

Picture in your mind Jesus with his disciples sitting perhaps as far from the rock cliff, temples, and gate of hell as possible, yet still seeing the top of the cliff, the rest hidden by the many trees growing along the stream in the area that helped form the headwaters of the Jordan River. "Who do people say the Son of Man is?" he asked them. When Peter made the confession that Jesus was the Messiah, Jesus replied, "Blessed are you, Simon son of Jonah! For this was not revealed to you by flesh and blood, but by My Father in heaven." He continued, "And I tell you, you are Peter, and on this rock I will build my church, and the gates of hell shall not prevail against it" (Matt. 16:18 ESV).

Let's focus on what Jesus said to Peter as they sat near the "gate of hell." When Peter confessed that Jesus was the Christ he replied that this was not revealed by flesh and blood, but by his Father in heaven. Jesus recognized the work in Peter of God's Spirit of wisdom and understanding as the revealer of truth—in this instance, that Jesus is the Messiah. It is interesting that Jesus states Peter is blessed to have this truth revealed to him. Think of the blessing of revelation that God imparts through his Spirit, including the entire revelation of the gospel of Jesus and the Word of God! My hope is that the Holy Spirit has given you the understanding that Jesus is our Savior and Messiah, and that we have great riches and abundance in our union with Christ.

In their letters to various churches, James and Paul teach us the importance of praying for wisdom and revelation. James, brother of Jesus and leader of the church in Jerusalem, wrote in his to-the-point manner, "Now if any of you lacks wisdom, he should ask God, who gives generously to all without finding fault, and it will be given to him" (James 1:5). What simple faith he calls on us to exercise: ask and it will be given to you! How often do we lack wisdom? How often is the Spirit of wisdom ready to give us what we need? As often as we lack wisdom, the Holy Spirit is ready to provide the wisdom of God.

Paul sends a beautiful prayer in his letter to the Ephesians:

> Remembering you in my prayers, that the God of our Lord Jesus Christ, the glorious Father, may give you a spirit of wisdom and revelation in your knowledge of Him. I ask that the eyes of your heart may be enlightened, so that you may know the hope of His calling, the riches of His glorious inheritance in the saints, and the surpassing greatness of His power to us who believe (Eph. 1:16–19).

How amazing that the same mighty power of God who raised Jesus from death to life can be ours through the Spirit who reveals to us the hope of the gospel; the riches we inherit as believers; and the great power we have through him.

The Spirit of Counsel and Might

> *I will bless the Lord who has given me counsel; My heart also instructs me in the night seasons.* NKJV
> PSALM 16:7

> *"But you will receive power when the Holy Spirit comes upon you."*
> ACTS 1:8

In my forty-year career in education, guidance counselors were always an important resource in the schools where I taught. My first year of teaching was in Mississippi; I was young and "green," standing outside the high school counselor's office one day, waiting to consult with her. A student came up and joined me, waiting to see the counselor as well. He started talking and I soon realized he thought I was a fellow student. I wasn't sure how to feel about that at the time! Now I would be flattered, but I would not be mistaken as a student at this stage of my life!

The greatest counselor is the Spirit of counsel and the Spirit of might that rested on Jesus. Those of us who have repented and received the gift of the Holy Spirit, as Peter preached, have this counselor and his might and power dwelling within us. When Jesus appointed seventy disciples to go out as laborers in the harvest, he told them to heal the sick and to say, "The kingdom of God has come near to you" (Luke 10:9). He had previously read from Isaiah (Luke 4) in the synagogue at Nazareth, "The Spirit of the Lord is on Me, because He has anointed Me to preach good news to the poor. He has sent Me to proclaim liberty to the captives and recovery of sight to the blind, to release the oppressed, to proclaim the year of the Lord's favor."

And now Jesus was sending the seventy to represent the kingdom of God, with the same anointing and power of Jesus by the Holy Spirit, to preach good news, proclaim liberty, heal, and release the oppressed. Because of their union with Jesus by the Holy Spirit, he instructed them, "Whoever listens to you listens to Me; whoever rejects you rejects Me; and whoever rejects Me rejects the One who sent Me" (Luke 10:16).

Matthew writes about a similar scenario at the judgment seat of Christ. He will set the sheep on this right, but the goats on his left. The King will declare those on his right are blessed and they will inherit the kingdom prepared for them from the foundation of the world because they gave him food when he was hungry and drink when he was thirsty. They took him in and clothed him, took care of him when he was sick, and visited him when he was in prison.

These righteous ones will ask him, "Lord, when did we see You hungry and feed You, or thirsty and give You something to drink? When did we see You a stranger and take You in, or naked and clothe You? When did we see You sick or in prison and visit You?"

And the King will reply, "Truly I tell you, whatever you did for one of the least of these brothers of Mine, you did for Me" (Matt. 25:33–40). Most of us would also be amazed at the idea that we ministered to Jesus when we helped a needy brother or sister. Jesus is so intimately united with the lowly and needy among us that our actions toward them are actions toward our Lord Jesus Christ himself. Sometimes, we are the needy and those who give us relief are giving relief to Jesus himself, and they will be rewarded because they were the righteous hands and feet of Jesus.

Do you remember Jesus, speaking from heaven, gave a similar message to Paul on the road to Damascus? When you persecute my followers, you persecute me. Instead of giving relief, Paul was persecuting those who were living in union with Christ Jesus.

Returning to the rest of the story about the seventy Jesus sent out, they returned with joy at the success of their mission. They felt the blessing that was anticipated in Psalm 84: "Blessed are those whose strength is in You.... They go from strength to strength, until each appears before God in Zion" (5, 7). This is a promise of strength, or power, that actually grows stronger and stronger with the presence of the Holy Spirit! Jesus also "rejoiced in the Holy Spirit" upon their return, and praised God, "because You have hidden these things from the wise and learned, and revealed them to little children" (Luke 10:21). Only the Holy Spirit has power to free captives of sin and impart purity and holiness in hearts. He has the power to do this and he delights to do this.

At the Last Supper, Jesus told his disciples four times (John 14:16, 26; John 15:26; John 16:7) that he would send "the Helper," *Paraklatos* in Greek, also translated Counselor, Advocate, or Comforter. He repeatedly assured them that he would come to them in the person of the Holy Spirit after he left them. As Advocate or Counselor, the Holy Spirit is compared to a legal advocate who is called to come alongside and plead another's cause before a judge as a defender or intercessor. The disciples needed an advocate and intercessor because as Jesus had just told them, "If you were of the world, it would love you as its own. Instead, the world hates you, because you are not of the world, but I have chosen you out of the world" (John 15:19). They needed the strength, counsel, and intercession of the Spirit of truth in order to be faithful witnesses to the gospel and to face the trials and persecutions they would suffer.

Jesus had faced trials and persecutions and understood the counsel and power of the Holy Spirit who led him into the wilderness to be tempted by the devil for forty days. As our example, Jesus opposed the devil with the Word of God, and the sword of the Spirit; the devil had no choice but to leave. In his triumph over the devil, Luke tells us, "Jesus returned to Galilee in the power of the Spirit, and the news about Him spread throughout the surrounding region. He taught in their synagogues and was glorified by everyone" (4:14–15). Jesus accomplished the purposes of God on earth with the help of the Holy Spirit. What a blessing that we share in this union when we are in Christ through the Holy Spirit! This is how we also can accomplish the purposes of God.

The Spirit of Knowledge and of the Fear of the Lord

> *The fear of the Lord is the beginning of wisdom, and knowledge of the Holy One is understanding.*
> PROVERBS 9:10

> *If you seek [wisdom] like silver and search it out like hidden treasure, then you will discern the fear of the Lord and discover the knowledge of God.*
> PROVERBS 2:4-5

When Jesus told the disciples he would come to them after he left the earth, it was because he knew God would send the Holy Spirit to dwell in them. He would be the same Spirit of the Lord that Isaiah spoke of. We have looked at Isaiah's revelation that God's Spirit resting on Jesus was the Spirit of the Lord, the Spirit of wisdom and understanding, and the Spirit of counsel and might. Finally, Isaiah says Jesus will have the Spirit of knowledge and of the fear of the Lord.

We usually think of fear in a negative way, and the Bible does speak of fear in this light; we are told "perfect love casts out fear" (1 John 4:18); on the other hand, it is appropriate to "fear the One who can destroy both soul and body in hell" (Matt. 10:28). Matthew here is speaking of a proper respect for the wrath and anger of God against evil and injustice. We know God is wholly righteous, and his Spirit of the fear of the Lord that rested on Jesus was righteous.

The fear of the Lord is the beginning of knowledge, and the beginning of wisdom according to Proverbs 1:7 and 9:10. It is important to God that we seek the fear and knowledge of the Lord. This is what David did when he said, "Teach me good judgment and knowledge, for I believe in Your commandments" (Ps. 119:66). We look to the example of Jesus to see the influence of the Spirit of knowledge and of the fear of the Lord in his life. Our goal is to pursue him in the same way that Jesus did.

It seems difficult to believe that Jesus had to learn anything, and yet the Bible tells us that as a young boy he "grew in wisdom and stature, and in favor with God and man" (Luke 2:52) and "though He was a Son, yet He learned obedience by the things which He suffered" (Heb. 5:8 NKJV). We can be sure his wisdom and learning came from his fear of the Lord.

What is the fear of the Lord? As a phrase, it is used mostly in the Old Testament and refers to reverence, admiration, love, awe of God, and additionally respect for the wrath of God. All of these attitudes come from knowing God in his fullness and lead to obedience to his will and his commandments. Certainly, we know Jesus revered, admired, respected, and was in awe of his Father. Isaiah adds to his prophecy of Isaiah 11:2, "He will delight in the fear of the Lord." Jesus obeyed the Father, even to laying down his life on the cross. Hebrews 9:14 says that it was through the Spirit that he offered Himself unblemished to God. In his flesh, "He had offered up prayers and supplications, with vehement cries and tears to Him who was able to save Him from death, and was heard because of His *godly fear*" (Heb. 5:7 emphasis mine).

Jesus prayed in the Garden of Gethsemane, "Father, if You are willing, take this cup from Me. Yet not My will, but Yours be done" (Luke 22:42). We know Jesus was heard because an angel from heaven appeared and strengthened him (Luke 22:43). God did not take away the cup of death on the cross, but when Jesus offered himself through the Spirit, his blood "[purified] our consciences from works of death, so that we may serve the living God!" (Heb. 9:14). Jesus' obedience satisfied God's requirement for forgiveness of sin and saved his followers from death! The writer of Hebrews exhorts us, "Therefore, since we are receiving a kingdom which cannot be shaken, let us have grace, by which we may serve God acceptably with reverence and *godly fear*" (Heb. 12:28 NKJV, emphasis mine). The Spirit of the fear of the Lord empowered Jesus to do the will of God at the most difficult time of his life and he will empower us to serve God throughout our lives.

The Bible is full of stories through which the Holy Spirit teaches reverence, awe, and love of God that lead to following his commandments. Here are some scenes from the Bible that inspire the fear of the Lord. Imagine yourself in the setting of these stories. What do you learn about God?

> The Lord God *(Yahweh Elohim)* drives Adam and Eve out of the garden and places cherubim with a flaming sword to guard the way of the tree of life. (Gen. 3:23–24)
>
> Moses stretches out his hand over the sea and the Lord causes a strong wind, which divides the sea. The children of Israel cross on dry ground. The waters form a wall on their right and on their left. (Ex. 14:21–22)
>
> A windstorm comes up on the Sea of Galilee. Jesus is asleep and the boat is filling with water. His disciples awaken him, and he rebukes the wind and the raging water. They cease, and there is a calm. (Luke 8: 22–25)
>
> The scribes and Pharisees have caught a woman in the act of adultery. They set her in the middle. Jesus says, ""Let him who is without sin among you be the first to cast a stone at her." One by one, they go out, leaving Jesus alone with the woman. Jesus declares, "I don't condemn you; now go and sin no more." (John 8:1–11)
>
> Jesus comes through the locked door where his disciples are. He tells Thomas to touch his hands and his side; "Do not be unbelieving but believe." Thomas answers, "My Lord and my God!" (John 20:26-29)

God's love, majesty, power, righteousness and justice that we see in these instances are still at work all around us. Sometimes, maybe often, we miss it. The remedy is to increase in our knowledge of God and his ways. The Spirit of knowledge helps us develop an intimate relationship with Jesus, so we don't miss seeing his hand at work; to do that, the Holy Spirit brings the life of Jesus to us and works his likeness in us. When Jesus was telling his disciples about the Holy Spirit's coming, he said that the Spirit of truth would guide them into all truth This is a promise for us as well. The Holy Spirit glorifies Jesus by revealing his truth to us (John 16:13–14).

In fact, God "has granted to us all things that pertain to life and godliness, through the knowledge of him who called us to his own glory and excellence" (2 Peter 1:3 ESV). How did God give us all the things we need to live a godly life? Yes, it is by knowing Jesus as our brother, our friend, Redeemer, Lord, our righteousness, and our strength. He has called us to his own glory and excellence. He grants us glory, excellence, and greatness as we live in union with him. There is nothing more that we need! We don't have to ask for more; we just take hold of what God has granted to us, and that comes through knowledge of who he is, imparted by the Holy Spirit and by the Word of God.

Jesus said the Spirit would guide us into *all* truth; Peter said God gives us "*all* things that pertain to life and godliness;" Paul prays that the Ephesians (and we!) be filled with *all* the fullness of God! Do you see that God does not hold back? He gives of his fullness without measure! Here is Paul's prayer:

> I ask that out of the riches of His glory He may strengthen you with power through His Spirit in your inner being, so that Christ may dwell in your hearts through faith. Then you, being rooted and grounded in love, will have power, together with all the saints, to comprehend the length and width and height and depth of the love of Christ, and to know this love that surpasses knowledge, that you may be filled with all the fullness of God (Eph. 3:16–19).

What a blessing to know we can know such depths of love and the fullness of God, filling our soul with the likeness of him, bearing his image in this world and beyond.

Contemplating His Ways

Do you feel united to Jesus by the Holy Spirit? How do you relate to the different attributes of the Holy Spirit: the Spirit of the Lord; the Spirit of wisdom and understanding; the Spirit of counsel and might; the Spirit of knowledge and of the fear of the Lord?

What experiences have you had that gave you a new reverence, admiration, love, awe of God, or respect for the wrath of God?

God has granted us all things that pertain to life and godliness according to 2 Peter 1:3 (ESV). How does that happen? This verse says "through the knowledge of him who called us to his own glory and excellence." Do you feel lacking sometimes in what you need in this life? Can we trust God to know what we need? How do we gain the knowledge of God? How do we answer God's call to partake of his glory, excellence, and godliness in our lives?

PART THREE

LIVING *in* UNION *with* JESUS

We saw in Part One that the Bible is a reliable source for showing that God's desire is that we live in union with him. Part Two outlines this union that is spiritual in nature. In Part Three we'll look at how we can live in the likeness of Jesus, being united through faith in him and his Word. Paul quotes Isaiah, "It is written, 'No eye has seen, no ear has heard, no heart has imagined, what God has prepared for those who love Him.' But God has revealed it to us by the Spirit. The Spirit searches all things, even the deep things of God. We have not received the spirit of the world, but the Spirit who is from God, that we may understand what God has freely given us" (1 Cor. 2:9–10, 12). We'll look at what God has given us through the Spirit, which enables us to live his likeness when we are connected as branches to the vine who is Christ Jesus. It is exciting to think we have a lifetime of learning the deep things of God!

CHAPTER 14

LIVING AS CHILDREN OF GOD

See how very much our Father loves us, for he calls us his children, and that is what we are!
I JOHN 3:1 NLT

For all who are led by the Spirit of God are sons of God.
ROMANS 8:14

All the guests had gone home. My granddaughter's sixth birthday party was over. We asked if it had met her expectations. With a twinkle in her eye, she said, "No!" then paused, threw her arms up, and exclaimed, "It was way better!" She had not known about all the fun planned, and the party turned out better than she expected.

We are safe to say life can be so much better than we expect because God delights in us; he has wonderful plans for each of us and gives us everything we need. Many of you know that heart-swelling delight when our children are joyful. God has given us such pleasure through our families. A prayer I like to pray for my grandchildren is from Psalm 90:14, "Oh, satisfy [them] early with Your mercy, that [they] may rejoice and be glad all [their] days!" (NKJV). We want our children and grandchildren to be satisfied with the love, mercy, and grace of Jesus from an early age so that they can be joyful, united to him all their days. We love them, want the best for them, and we work to not only teach them, but show them by example the way to live as children of God.

It is no different for God the Father. He sent Jesus to take our sins upon himself, and then to teach us the way to live a joy-filled life. Isaiah said, "All your children shall be taught by the Lord, and great shall be the peace of your children" (Is. 54:13 NKJV). Jesus quoted Isaiah when he said, "It is written in the Prophets: 'And they will all be taught by God.' Everyone who has heard the Father and learned from Him comes to Me" (John 6:45). In these verses, Isaiah and then Jesus show that when we learn about and truly know God, he will reveal the truth of his Son to us and to our children after us. This repeated thread joins the Old Testament with the New and is a beautiful way God shows us the reliability of his Word and his promises made through the prophets.

BECOMING GOD'S CHILDREN

God has shown us that we are his children, united to him as his family. How did that happen? Paul writes that God chose us for adoption as sons through Jesus, who paid the ultimate price to reconcile us to God as his children. "But to all who did receive Him, to those who believed in His name, He gave the right to become children of God, children born not of blood, nor of the desire or will of man, but born of God" (John 1:12–13).

In the moving scene at the garden tomb, Mary Magdalene wept when she saw that Jesus' body was missing. Jesus appeared to her and said, "Go and tell My brothers, 'I am ascending to My Father and your Father, to My God and your God'" (John 20:17). Jesus expresses the ultimate union with him that we could ever hope for! He is our brother, his Father is our Father, and his God is our God. In a blessed mirror of Jesus' relationship to the Father, we are sons and daughters of God. With the same Father and the same God, we are brothers and sisters of Christ Jesus. This relationship is formed in love, and made possible through Jesus' obedience to come to earth to die for the sins of his family. This is expressed in

Hebrews 2:17; "[Jesus] had to be made like His brothers in every way, so that He might become a merciful and faithful high priest in service to God, in order to make atonement for the sins of the people."

Along with the Father and Jesus, the Holy Spirit has a role in bringing us into the family. The Spirit, who raised Jesus from the dead, dwells within and gives us life; we are no longer destined to eternal death. Those who are led by the Spirit are sons of God. "The Spirit Himself bears witness with our spirit that we are children of God, and if children, then heirs—heirs of God and joint heirs with Christ, if indeed we suffer with *Him*, that we may also be glorified together" (Rom. 8:11–17 NKJV). And "God has poured out His love into our hearts through the Holy Spirit, whom He has given us" (Rom. 5:5). This is the steadfast love of our Father that never ceases!

Sometimes we have to assure our children that they are safe and that we will not abandon them. The house may get quiet and your child fears that they are left alone. You reassure them that you will never leave them; you love them, and they are important. Or don't you love it when a child reaches for your hand, feeling unsure about their surroundings? We adults are not so different. Jesus must have realized that his disciples, his brothers, were anxious when he sent them out to give witness of him. He reassured them that God kept track of every sparrow that fell to the ground, and they were of much more value to him than many sparrows. In fact, he knew exactly how many hairs were on their heads (Matt. 10:29–31). How dear would each one be to God for him to know that? God has seen some of us experience the hair count going down over the years!

Jesus also taught that we should not have an anxious mind about what we will wear, or eat, or drink; "These things dominate the thoughts of unbelievers all over the world, but your Father already knows your needs. Seek the Kingdom of God above all else, and he will give you everything you need. So don't be afraid, little flock. For it gives your Father great happiness to give you the Kingdom" (Luke 12:30–32 NLT). What an endearing reminder Jesus gives us, his little flock: "Your Father" is greatly happy to give you the kingdom--righteousness, peace, and joy in the Holy Spirit. Jesus taught what our loving Father is like and how we can relate to him as sons and daughters. When Jesus says "your Father," he speaks of his Father as well.

JESUS' INTERCESSORY PASSOVER PRAYER

In Jesus' intercessory prayer to God to close the last Passover feast, we see a clear illustration of the love, protection, and care that both the Father and the Son have for us as part of their family. Jesus is perfectly one with his Father, and in his prayer he expressed the sacred responsibility he felt to shepherd "those whom you have given me." He referred to these ones God gave him seven times in twenty-three verses in his John 17 prayer. In using this phrase, it is certain that Jesus shows that he himself fulfilled Isaiah's prophecy, "Here am I, and the children the Lord has given me" (Is. 8:18). This Old Testament prophecy is quoted again in the New Testament book of Hebrews, along with three other Old Testament prophecies in the same passage that Jesus fulfilled. In this Hebrews 2 passage below, the writer records Jesus' actions as God's Son and representative. Notice all the references to family here:

> In bringing many *sons* to glory, it was fitting for God, for whom and through whom all things exist, to make the author of their salvation perfect through suffering. For both the One who sanctifies and those who are sanctified are of the same *family* [*from one Father* NASB]. So Jesus is not ashamed to call them *brothers*. He says:
> "I will proclaim Your name to My *brothers*; [Prophecy from Ps. 22]
> I will sing Your praises in the assembly." [from Ps. 22]
> And again: "I will put My trust in Him." [from Is. 8]
> And once again: "Here am I, and *the children God has given Me*" [from Is. 8:18]
> (Heb. 2:10–13, emphasis mine).

It is God who has called us to be his family as sons and daughters, to share in the glory of union with him. This is possible only through the suffering of his Son, Jesus, who took our sin upon himself so that we receive his life and his honor (John 5:44). We have become part of the family of God as sons and daughters, and brothers and sisters of Jesus.

Jesus summarizes his life work and aim is to show his family who the Father is and how he loves them. He ends his Passover prayer in John 17: "And I have made Your name known to them and will continue to make it known, so that the love You have for Me may be in them, and I in them" (v. 26). Jesus affirms here that he fulfilled the Psalm 22:22 prophecy, "I will proclaim Your name to My brothers." Did you notice that in his prayer, Jesus told his Father he would continue to make him known? He knew he would soon be leaving his disciples to go back to the glories of heaven. How would he continue to make God known? Yes, he was sending his Holy Spirit whom we spoke of in the last chapter. This is why earlier that evening he said, "I will come to you," indicating his Spirit would come to live in us. In this ending of his prayer, Jesus also revealed in this twenty-sixth verse that his aim for his followers was that God love them the same way he loved Jesus: "So that the love You have for Me may be in them, and I in them." These statements are amazing, but there is so much more in this beautiful prayer, which comprises the entire seventeenth chapter.

Do you see here the family love, loyalty, care, and responsibility Jesus and the Father feel toward "those who will believe in me" (17:20), which includes you and me today? Using the word "keep" or "kept," sometimes translated "protect," five times during his prayer, Jesus' thoughts center on the future protection of his brothers and sisters. His petitions and declarations include:

> "They were Yours, You gave them to Me, and they have *kept* Your word" (v. 6).
>
> "*Keep* through Your name those whom You have given me" (v. 11).

"While I was with them in the world, I *kept* them in Your name. Those whom You gave Me I have *kept*" (v. 12).
"[I pray] that you should *keep* them from the evil one" (v. 15 NKJV, emphasis mine).

Jesus' petitions show he wants his followers to have the same relationship with the Father as he has: "If you keep My commandments, you will remain in My love, just as I have kept My Father's commandments and remain in His love" (John 15:10). In keeping Jesus' commandments, we remain in his love in the way Jesus remained in the Father's love. Earlier teachings of Jesus echo his desire to keep his followers together as his little flock: "No one can snatch them out of My hand" (John 10:29); and "I shall lose none of those He has given Me, but raise them up at the last day" (John 6:39). Paul echoes this idea that God cares for us as family: "You belong to Christ, and Christ belongs to God" (1 Cor. 3:23).

Jesus also prays for those that will believe in him in the future, "That all of them may be one, as You, Father, are in Me, and I am in You. May they also be in Us, so that the world may believe that You sent Me" (17:21). Our unity with other believers is because of our shared union with Christ, through him union with the Father, and the shared indwelling of the Holy Spirit. Our union with one another witnesses to the world that we are disciples of Jesus Christ, who is the power of God and the wisdom of God (1 Cor. 1:24).

Additionally in this Passover prayer, Jesus petitions God that his followers have the joy that he himself has (v. 13, 16); that the Father keep them from the evil one (v. 15); that they become more like him (v. 11); that they be holy and set apart for service to God (v. 17–19); receiving the glory that Jesus has (v. 22); and that they be with him where he is and see the glory he had from the Father before the foundation of the world (v. 24). Do you think God is answering this great, even startling prayer? He certainly is! In the coming chapters we'll see many other ways that today God is answering Jesus' prayer that he dwell in us, keep and protect us, and that God's love, joy, and glory be in us. All through the Bible we see ways that God answers this prayer as his very life comes into our spirits so we can live the likeness of Jesus.

MATURING

We are often amazed how quickly little ones grow. I have even teased my grandchildren that I want to put a brick on their heads to keep them from getting so big. And no, you are not almost as tall as I am! Yet it seems every time I see them, they have changed and matured in some way, however small. We adults tend to think we don't need to grow up and mature. We have been there and done that. But what about changing and maturing day by day in our faith? Paul had much to say about growing up and maturing as individuals and as members of the body of Christ, his church. In his New Testament letters to various churches that he ministered to, he often addressed problems of false teaching in the church that result in error of belief and behavior; even today his letters bring encouragement and warning for believers. For example, he says, "Brothers and *sisters*, do not be children in your thinking; yet in evil be infants, but in your thinking be mature" (1 Cor. 14:20 NASB).

We'll see that Peter and Paul both deliver the message that we need to grow in the grace and knowledge of our Lord Jesus Christ. Peter reminds his readers of what he feels essential for "those who ... have received a faith as precious as ours" (2 Peter 1:1). He writes:

> But the Day of the Lord will come like a thief. The heavens will disappear with a roar, the elements will be destroyed by fire, and the earth and its works will be laid bare.
>
> Since everything will be destroyed in this way, what kind of people ought you to be? You ought to conduct yourselves in holiness and godliness. . . . But in keeping with God's promise, we are looking forward to a new

heaven and a new earth, where righteousness dwells. Therefore, beloved, as you anticipate these things, make every effort to be found at peace—spotless and blameless in His sight (2 Peter 3:10–11, 13–14).

The destruction of the earth and its works at the final judgment is the motivation for us to be mature, spotless, and blameless, looking forward to heaven where only righteousness dwells.

In Ephesians, Paul sets essentially this same goal for the body of Christ:

> "[that] we all come to such unity in our faith and knowledge of God's Son that we will be mature [perfect, complete] in the Lord, measuring up to the full and complete standard of Christ. Then we will no longer be immature like children. We won't be tossed and blown about by every wind of new teaching…. Instead, we will speak the truth in love, growing in every way more and more like Christ, who is the head of his body, the church" (Eph. 4:13–15 NLT).

Our goal is to mature as believers together in the church in order to be transformed into the likeness of Christ with increasing glory, forming the complete body of Christ, who is the head. In order to do that, we need to unify in the principles of our faith and our belief in the work of the Son of God. The goal is to grow up as the body of Jesus, to work together as one perfect, complete man to reach the full measure of Christ, the head who controls the body. We all have distinct functions within the body like the members of our physical body do, but as members of the body of Christ, we share one life, the life of Jesus. His life supplies us with all we need to be a complete, mature body that functions in the full and complete standard of Christ Jesus, our head, as we grow together in the grace and in the love that flows from him.

Contemplating His Ways

Matthew 26, Mark 14, and Luke 22 record what Jesus said in offering the bread and the wine at his last Passover. We discussed his teachings that night from John 13 to 17. Next time you take communion, imagine yourself in the upper room at Passover with Jesus. What is the mood in the room? As he speaks, what strikes your heart? How does Jesus want to change you?

How has God answered Jesus' John 17 prayer in your life?

As heirs of God and joint heirs with Christ, we have an inheritance, or portion. What does this mean? In Psalm 73:26, the psalmist declares, "My flesh and my heart may fail, but God is the strength of my heart and my portion forever." Use your search engine to do a study of our spiritual inheritance. The parable of the lost son points in this direction. It ends with this statement of the father, "All that is mine is yours." (Luke 15:31). See also I Peter 1:3–4.

CHAPTER 15

FORMING JESUS WITHIN

*Do you not know that you yourselves are God's temple,
and that God's Spirit dwells in you?*
1 CORINTHIANS 3:16

*We are God's fellow workers; you are God's field,
God's building.*
1 CORINTHIANS 3:9

GOD'S BUILDING

One of the most awe-inspiring, even miraculous things I saw in Israel, was a stone. That doesn't sound so impressive, but let me explain. This stone and the country as a whole, helped me understand Psalm 102:14 written about Jerusalem, "Your servants take pleasure in her stones, and show favor to her dust" (NKJV).

It is called the Great Stone, and it is part of the retaining wall, which served to stabilize the mountain top platform for the Second Temple built by Herod the Great on Mount Moriah. This revered mountain where God provided a ram for Abraham to sacrifice instead of his only son Isaac, has been built up over the years, and fortified to provide building space, first for Solomon's temple, then Zerubbabel's rebuilt temple, and finally Herod's temple of Jesus' day. This is the most sacred site in Judaism, and visited by millions each year. Today you can take an underground tour to see the stones, which were placed on bedrock, but because the city was built up over years, this base of the wall is now the underground part of the expanse of the Western Wall. As you walk along the underground tunnel alongside this wall, your guide stops at the Great Stone. The sheer magnitude of it is overwhelming, and hard to put into words. It was 20 feet above the Herodian street level, 44 feet long, 11.5 feet high, and estimated to be 7 to 15 feet deep, and weigh several hundred tons. It stands out far and above as the grandest, most impressive stone that stabilizes the western wall of the temple mount.

It is hard to move on down the tunnel away from the presence of this monumental stone that leaves you with a sense of awe as if you were in the presence of a representation of the greatness and power of God. Some Bible scholars have suggested that Isaiah referred to this stone when he wrote, "So this is what the Lord God says: 'See, I lay a stone in Zion, a tested stone, a precious cornerstone, a sure foundation; the one who believes will never be shaken'" (28:16). There can be little doubt after studying New Testament references to foundations, that this verse is a prophecy about Jesus. The Great Stone is a massive reminder of the greatness and power of Jesus, the sure and eternal foundation God provided for the salvation of his people on earth.

We can compare maturing in faith to building on a strong foundation. In the last chapter we spoke of Paul's comparison of growing and maturing in Christ to a complete body that functions together with Christ as the head. In a similar illustration of how our lives are joined to him, Jesus spoke of himself as the cornerstone on which individually and together as his church, we are built up as God's building. Jesus accused the chief priests and elders of rejecting his teaching and authority, and revealed that it was he who was the stone the builders rejected that had become the cornerstone as the Scriptures prophesied in Psalm 118 (Matt. 21:42).

Jesus ended his Sermon on the Mount with the parable of two builders. He said whoever hears what he has said and does them is like the wise man who built his house on the rock so that it withstood the floods and winds; on the other hand, whoever does not hear and do his sayings is like the foolish man who built his house on the sand. When the floods and winds came, his house fell (Matt. 7:24-27). This reminds me of the microburst that blew the farrowing house for mother sows and piglets off its foundation on the Missouri farm where I grew up. It was totally useless and had to be torn down. We cannot separate ourselves from Jesus, our foundation!

Similarly, we cannot separate ourselves from the church, the body of Christ, because together we are built up with other believers into a dwelling place for God in His Spirit. A real challenge in Paul's day was for Jews to accept Gentiles into the young church. Paul tells the Gentile Ephesians that they have been made one in Christ Jesus with the Jews who believed in Jesus, and so both have access by one Spirit to the Father. He continued in Ephesians 2:19-21, "Therefore you are no longer strangers and foreigners [Jews and Gentiles], but fellow citizens with the saints and members of God's household, built on the foundation of the apostles and prophets, with Christ Jesus Himself as the cornerstone. In Him the whole building is fitted together and grows into a holy temple in the Lord." In their union with one another, and with Jesus Christ, they are the true dwelling place of the Most High God. The same is true for us in the church of Jesus Christ today.

We may not face division between Jews and Gentiles in the way the first century church did, but we need to fit together in unity with other believers and as Peter said, "As you come to Him, the living stone, rejected by men but chosen and precious in God's sight, you also, like living stones, are being built into a spiritual house to be a holy priesthood, ... acceptable to God through Jesus Christ" (1 Peter 2:4-5).

There are warnings in the Bible about how we as individuals build on the foundation of Christ. The idea is not to start building and quit, delay, or perhaps use materials or lifestyles that are not worthy of God's building. I am reminded of concrete block homes in Jordan today that are one or two stories high, but have metal rods sticking up above the highest floor in anticipation of adding another story when a family member gets married. It certainly doesn't add to the appeal of the house, and makes the neighborhood look like a collection of unfinished houses. This is not something we want our lives and the body of Christ, the temple of the Lord, to look like!

We are to continue to build in our knowledge of God, and not be content with a foundation of elementary principles of God. The writer of Hebrews said one way to build to maturity is to train our senses to distinguish good from evil (Heb. 5:14). In a similar way, Jude says the way to recognize false teaching that can damage your building is to "[Build] yourselves up in your most holy faith and praying in the Holy Spirit, keep yourselves in the love of God," (vv. 20–21 ESV). He told the believing church members that building themselves up in their faith is essential for exposing untruth and progressing in godliness.

Our faith in God is the foundation for everything in our lives. It takes us off the throne and allows God to rule in our hearts; this unity with him gives us the power to practice his righteousness. God has laid the foundation of faith and we then build on that foundation. He warns us to be careful how we build on it:

> For no one can lay a foundation other than the one already laid, which is Jesus Christ. If anyone builds on this foundation using gold, silver, precious stones, wood, hay, or straw, his workmanship will be evident, because the Day will bring it to light. It will be revealed with fire, and the fire will prove the quality of each man's work. If what he has built survives, he will receive a reward. If it is burned up, he will suffer loss. He himself will be saved, but only as if through the flames" (1 Cor. 3:11–15).

This is a warning that we must be careful how we build. There are many possibilities for foundations in our lives; maybe it's wealth, career, or education, but because of our trust and faith in God, he gives us the power to build wisely on the foundation of Jesus Christ, with gold, silver, and precious stones that represent obedience to his truth. Paul prayed a powerful prayer for the church in Colosse, "We have not stopped praying for you and asking God to fill you with the knowledge of His will in all spiritual wisdom and understanding, so that you may walk in a manner worthy of the Lord and may please Him in every way: bearing fruit in every good work, growing in the knowledge of God" (Col. 1:9–10). Paul's prayer lays out what Jude calls building yourselves up in your faith: increasing in the knowledge of God's will in spiritual wisdom and understanding; living worthy of the Lord; pleasing him; bearing fruit in good works; and growing in the knowledge of God. Sometimes we struggle to think this is possible, but this prayer shows us not only is it possible, but God will accomplish this for us when we ask him to. What a beautiful way to pray for others as well.

FORMING CHRIST WITHIN

My little children, for whom I am again in the
anguish of childbirth until Christ is formed in you!
GALATIANS 4:19 ESV

Paul uses a very striking comparison in the above verse to the pains of childbirth and how he feels toward the young churches under his care. Even if you haven't experienced the pain of childbirth, you have an idea how intense it is. So, Paul feels that degree of involvement, responsibility, even anguish, for Christ to be formed in "those sanctified in Christ Jesus and called to be holy" (1 Cor. 1:2). As the body of Christ, who is the head, they are being built into a spiritual house, or as Paul said, Christ is being formed in them. What does that mean? It is God delighting to work out the likeness of his Son in union with those sanctified by the blood sacrifice of Jesus.

In most of his New Testament letters to different churches, Paul expresses great concern about issues and behaviors that do not reflect the likeness of Jesus. When he addresses the Galatians, he even says he experiences pain as of childbirth "until Christ is formed in you! I wish I could be present with you now and change my tone, for I am perplexed about you" (4:19–20 ESV). The Galatian church continued to be enslaved to the law, thinking their salvation comes by their works instead of by faith in Jesus. Paul begins his letter to them, "I am amazed how quickly you are deserting the One who called you by the grace of Christ and are turning to a different gospel" (1:6). He continues, "O foolish Galatians! Who has bewitched you? Before your very eyes Jesus Christ was clearly portrayed as crucified. I would like to learn just one thing from you: Did you receive the Spirit by works of the law, or by hearing with faith?" (3:1–2).

In other warnings and exhortations, Paul appeals to the Corinthians to put aside divisions among themselves and be united in mind and conviction. In Titus he says many in the church at Crete are rebellious and full of empty talk and deception, teaching things they should not (1:10–11). Similarly, he tells the Colossians, "I want you to know how much I am struggling for you and for those at Laodicea . . . that they may be encouraged in heart, knit together in love, and filled with the full riches of complete understanding, so that they may know the mystery of God, namely Christ" (2:1-3); in other words, Paul wanted the newly revealed mystery of the gospel of Jesus, to be formed in them, filling them with his spiritual riches.

Put Off the Old Man

> *Put off, concerning your former conduct, the old man which grows corrupt according to the deceitful lusts.*
> EPHESIANS 4:22 (NKJV)

When Paul tells the churches what he sees and hears that reveals Christ is not yet formed in them, he describes the "old man," and then how the "new man," created in the image of God, forms the likeness of Jesus within so that he is alive in Christ, hidden in him, and complete in union with him.

When we are hidden in Christ and formed in his likeness, we will be followers of God as dear children, walking in love as Christ loved us, not grieving the Holy Spirit who has been given to us as a guarantee of eternal life with God. If you have heard and been taught by Jesus, and known his truth, you will put to death your earthly nature, the old unredeemed man whose understanding is darkened, alienated from the life of God because of ignorance and hardening of heart.

Paul is very clear to define walking in darkness instead of in light. It is foolish talking, coarse jesting, fornication, sexual immorality, covetousness, which is idolatry, anger, and malice, to name a few of the unfruitful works of darkness. He says do not lie to one another or have fellowship with darkness but rather expose it in the light of Christ. Don't walk as fools but as the wise, making the most of your time because the days are evil. Instead of being drunk with wine, be filled with the Spirit! All this means putting off your former way of life before becoming a new creation in Christ (Eph. 4, 5, Col. 3).

Put On the New Man

> *Put on the new self, created to be like God*
> *in true righteousness and holiness.*
> EPHESIANS 4:24

Last words are important. The final sermons of an outgoing pastor, or the last letter a Bible author writes will likely contain valuable life lessons. I will never forget the theme of a last sermon in my church; it was to contemplate and meditate on the cross of Christ as the central truth of God. Everything in life flows from the cross, including how we treat each other. The pastor had us stand up and work together to memorize Ephesians 4:32: "Be kind to one another, tenderhearted, forgiving one another, even as God in Christ forgave you" (NKJV). The kind, tenderhearted, and forgiving are those in whom Christ has been formed.

Tradition gives us a picture of the last words Peter spoke to his wife who died for her faith before he did. Clement of Rome, first century church leader who was likely taught the Christian faith by Peter and Paul, wrote this about her martyrdom.

> They say that the blessed Peter when he saw his own wife led out to death rejoiced at her calling and at her return home and called out to her in true warning and comfort, addressing her by her name, "Remember the Lord." Such was the marriage of the blessed and the perfect disposition of those dearest to them (*Ecclesiastical History*, 3.30.2).[1]

I wept when I saw this. The last words she knew she would ever hear from her powerful, loving husband were so critically comforting to her who had faithfully and lovingly traveled with and supported him in his ministry to young churches, and who above all, loved and followed Jesus (Matt. 8:14–15 and 1 Cor. 9:5).

When Peter wrote his last letter, he gave a description of the new man. What message did he want to leave with those who would read it after his death? He knew much about the formation of Christ within. Here is what he said:

> His divine power has granted to us all things that pertain to life and godliness, through the knowledge of him who called us to his own glory and excellence, by which he has granted to us his precious and very great promises, so that through them you may become partakers of the divine nature, having escaped from the corruption that is in the world because of sinful desire. For this very reason, make every effort to supplement your faith with virtue and

virtue with knowledge, and knowledge with self-control, and self-control with steadfastness, and steadfastness with godliness, and godliness with brotherly affection, and brotherly affection with love.

For if these qualities are yours and are increasing, they keep you from being ineffective or unfruitful in the knowledge of our Lord Jesus Christ.... For in this way there will be richly provided for you an entrance into the eternal kingdom of our Lord and Savior Jesus Christ (2 Peter 1:3–8, 11 ESV).

Peter is looking forward to his soon entrance into the kingdom of his Lord who had lovingly formed this strong, impulsive, sometimes rash man into his effective, fruitful follower. The remembrance of being cleansed and forgiven of former sins leads to faith, virtue, knowledge, self-control, steadfastness, godliness, brotherly affection (Greek, *philadelphia*), and love *(agape)*. God's power working in us grants these virtues listed here, each building on and perfecting the previous, finally producing the *agape* love of God himself.

The last words of Peter's letter are a warning to not fall from steadfastness and be susceptible to error, "But grow in the grace and knowledge of our Lord and Savior Jesus Christ. To Him be the glory both now and to the day of eternity. Amen" (2 Peter 3:18).

It is possible to grow in grace because at the moment of salvation, the seed of God's divine nature is implanted in our hearts, as 2 Peter 1:4 above tells us, empowering the chain of virtues Peter outlines. Alexander MacLaren writes about the "bold words" of the verse: "He has given us His precious and magnificent promises, so that through them you may become partakers of the divine nature, now that you have escaped the corruption in the world caused by evil desires." MacLaren comments:

> Bold as they are...they are only putting into other language the teaching of which the whole New Testament

is full, that men may, and do, by their faith, receive into their spirits a real communication of the life of God. What else does the language about being "the sons and daughters of the Lord Almighty" mean?... What else mean Christ's frequent declarations that He dwells in us and we in Him, as the branch in the vine, as the members in the body?... Do not all teach that in some most real sense the very purpose of Christianity, for which God has sent His Son, and His Son has come, is that we, poor, sinful, weak, limited, ignorant creatures as we are, may be lifted up into that solemn and awful elevation, and receive in our trembling and yet strengthened souls a spark of God? It means that into us may come the very God Himself.

More and more of God we may receive every day we live, and through the endless ages of eternity. . . . He who becomes partaker of the Divine nature can never die. So as Christ taught us the great argument for immortality is the present relation between God and us.[2]

Paul also described the new self to be formed within, as being "created to be like God in true righteousness and holiness" (Eph. 4:24). He gives a picture of the new man in Colossians 3. It is a picture of the holy and beloved of the Lord. They set their minds on things above, not on things of the earth, because they have died, and their life is hidden with Christ in God. He urges them to do this:

> Therefore, as the elect of God, holy and beloved, clothe yourselves with hearts of compassion, kindness, humility, gentleness, and patience. Bear with one another and forgive any complaint you may have against someone else. Forgive as the Lord forgave you. And over all these virtues put on love *[agape]*, which is the bond of perfect unity.

Let the peace of Christ rule in your hearts, for to this you were called as members of one body. And be thankful (Col. 3:12-15).

The virtues and the Word of Christ should abide within each member of the body of Christ. He lists these virtues here which are the very qualities of Jesus: compassion, kindness, humility, gentleness, patience, peace, and above all, love which binds together the elect of God. We are to forgive as Christ forgave. Jesus is formed in us to the degree we allow the character of God and his Word to abide in our hearts and minds. Let us "Remember the Lord" without ceasing.

Contemplating His Ways

How do you put off the old man and put on the new man? Read I Corinthians 2:6-16 and 3:1. Highlight or count the words spirit, Spirit, spiritual. What are two or three themes Paul is writing about? How do they relate to maturity, the formation of Christ within and union with him?

How would you rate yourself on a scale of 1 (nearsighted and blind) to 10 (the excellence and glory of Jesus Christ) on each quality Peter defines for being effective and fruitful in the knowledge of Jesus Christ: faith, virtue, knowledge, self-control, steadfastness, godliness, brotherly affection, and love? How does the grace of God support you in growing in these virtues?

CHAPTER 16

LIVING IN THE FREEDOM OF JESUS

> *Where the Spirit of the Lord is present, there is freedom. All of us, then, reflect the glory of the Lord with uncovered faces; and that same glory, coming from the Lord, who is the Spirit, transforms us into his likeness in an ever greater degree of glory.*
> 2 CORINTHIANS 3:17–18, GNT

A few months after Evan went to heaven, I learned a lesson about how change in life can lead to freedom in Jesus. (I smile because that's what he used to say to help people remember his name, "Evan going to heaven.") I met my sisters in Colorado to see the quaking aspens turn their beautiful fall colors. I had to get the T-shirt, so I found one with beautiful yellow-gold aspens on the front. In small letters, it said, "Change Is Good." I immediately thought of the huge change that the loss of my husband had brought to my life. How could it be good? And yet, I felt a God-tug and thought, "Okay, I'm open to see how this change can be good."

God began to turn my mind from grief and sadness to being open to the goodness of his presence in my life and all the love and hope he wanted to give me for my future. It wasn't long after that, that God spoke to me through Ecclesiastes 7:10: "Say not, 'Why were the former days better than these?' For it is not from wisdom that you ask this" (ESV). I was so grateful to God for renewing my mind and showing me this truth that because I was sheltered in him, every day could be better than the previous, no matter what the circumstances. In fact, Paul wrote that as we reflect the glory of the Lord, we are being changed, or transformed, into his likeness with an ever increasing degree of glory (2 Cor. 3:18). Changes that bring pain to our lives can turn into the change that makes us more like the glorious image of the Lord when we act on the truth that we have a firm and secure hope in him as an anchor for our soul.

Another change was around the corner for me. The lesson I learned about trust in God's faithfulness through the grief of losing Evan, gave me strength and hope in facing the challenge of a cancer fight. God miraculously preserved my life and through it all he proved that when I set the Lord before me, and realize he is at my right hand, I cannot be shaken, as David said in Psalm 16. I experienced what he said next, "Therefore my heart is glad and my whole being rejoices; my body also rests securely" (vv. 8–9 CSB). This is living in the freedom, joy, and safety of Jesus every day as we walk in union with him. Let's take a look at God's plan for our freedom in Christ.

FREEDOM FROM BONDAGE TO SIN AND DEATH

> *For in Christ Jesus the law of the Spirit of life set you free from the law of sin and death.*
> ROMANS 8:2

The Israelites' exodus from Egypt is a major salvation theme in the Bible, foreshadowing redemption through Jesus. The Jewish holiday of Passover commemorates this exodus. In the Haggadah, the guide to the Passover seder feast, there is a line that says that in every generation, each person must see himself as if he came out of Egypt. Everyone should see himself every day of the year, especially at Passover, as someone who has been redeemed, meaning he was freed from Egypt, a free man to start a new life. Like the Israelites who escaped from Egypt to eventually enter the Promised Land, believers in Jesus have been redeemed and enter into the promised eternal life of Jesus. We have been freed from the bondage of sin and death, having been born again to a living hope. We praise God for his deliverance along with the Israelites who sang the song of Moses when they saw the destruction of the Egyptian army, "With your unfailing love you lead the people you have redeemed. . . . whom you have purchased" (Ex. 15:13, 16 NLT).

My husband told a modern-day redemption story about Killian, a man he met on an island in Lake Victoria in Kenya. Killian was a murderer, thief, drug abuser, drug seller, and all-around bad guy. My husband wrote this about him:

> He heard about our meetings where I was teaching another group about walking in the supernatural and came because his lungs were diseased by the drug use. I didn't know who this man was; I just knew they rather avoided him. I laid my hand on his chest and cried to the Lord to heal, but not only heal, but take everything out that didn't belong and cleanse all that was wrong and evil. Something very potent happened to Killian. That night he gave his testimony. He said that when he came, he only wanted healing, but when the white man placed his hand on him and spoke, all manner of evil left him in a rush, and he met God.[3]

Killian returned to the meeting that evening a transformed man. He lay at the front of the meeting place, his face in the dirt, humbled before God and all the people who knew his evil background. He had felt the evil that ruled his life washed away by God and stood before his acquaintances a man freed from the chains of sin, with new life in Jesus.

Killian started on a path to transformation into the likeness of Jesus. This is the path of the Lord where "the Spirit, transforms us into his likeness in an ever greater degree of glory" (2 Cor. 3:18 GNT). In this verse, the

Greek word *metamorphóō*, related to our English verb metamorphose, is used for transform; Merriam Webster defines *metamorphose*, "to change strikingly the appearance or character of." The Greek literally says, transformed after being with, or transfigured. What power and freedom there is in knowing that after being with the Spirit of Jesus, we are increasingly metamorphosed, transformed, or transfigured into his glorious likeness!

Killian, as well as the Israelites, drank from the spiritual rock, and that rock was Christ (1 Cor. 10:4). Just as the waters from the rock provided a constant supply in the wilderness during the exodus from Egypt, so the grace, goodness and mercy of Jesus follow his children all the days of their lives. It is a supply of freedom from bondage to sin.

Sadly, many Israelites did not hold fast to their Redeemer after the exodus. Paul writes that even though God supplied them with food and water in the wilderness, they became examples that we should not follow. They lusted after evil things, became idolaters, committed sexual immorality, tempted Christ, and complained; against all of which Paul warns his readers.

Similarly, the writer of Hebrews warns against unbelief in departing from the living God, and that we should instead encourage one another lest any be hardened through the deceitfulness of sin. The promise is, "For we have become partakers of Christ if we hold the beginning of our confidence steadfast to the end" (Heb. 3:14 NKJV). In partaking of Christ, we are partakers of his Spirit, his grace, his righteousness, and his very life. Barnes comments, "The idea is, that we participate in all that pertains to him. It is a union of feeling and affection; a union of principle and of congeniality; a union of dependence as well as love; a union where nothing is to be imparted by us, but everything gained."[4] Paul states very clearly in Romans 6:23, "The wages of sin is death, but the gift of God is eternal life *in Christ Jesus our Lord*" (emphasis mine).

Jesus came to offer freedom from slavery to sin. When he left Galilee for the last time to go up to Jerusalem before his death, he talked openly to the Jews about doing the will of his Father. They marveled, asking, "How has this man become learned, not having been educated?"; "Have the rulers truly recognized that this is the Christ [the Messiah]?"; "When the Christ comes, will He perform more signs than this man?" and finally they asked, "Who are you?" (John 7:15, 26, 31; 8:25).

In answer to their questions, Jesus said, "I do nothing on My own, but speak exactly what the Father has taught Me" (John 8:28). At this and other teachings of his, many of the people believed in Him, knowing he was telling them he was the Son of God, the Messiah. Jesus had a warning for these new believers: "If you continue in My word, you are truly My disciples. Then you will know the truth, and the truth will set you free. . . . Truly, truly, I tell you, everyone who sins is a slave to sin. . . . If the Son sets you free, you will be free indeed" (John 8:31-32, 34, 36).

To those who follow his teachings, Jesus grants true freedom from the slavery of sin. This is the fulfillment of Isaiah's prophecy, "I am the Lord, I have called You in righteousness ... to bring out prisoners from the dungeon and those who dwell in darkness from the prison;" and again, "The Spirit of the Lord God is upon me ... He has sent me to bind up the brokenhearted, to proclaim release to captives and freedom to prisoners" (Is. 42:6-7; 61:1).

Later, at Passover Jesus adds more on this theme explaining the life he offers to those captives who have been released; If we abide [continue] in him, and his words abide in us, we are abiding in the love of Jesus, just as he abides in his Father's love and follows his commandments. Jesus wants us to be free indeed, in a union of love with him as he is in a union of love with his Father. These things Jesus tells us that we might have fullness of joy. In fact, Jesus said it was his own joy that would be in us and for that reason, our joy will be complete because his is complete (John 15:7-11).

Truly, to be freed from slavery is cause for joy. A church in my area has purchased the freedom of entire Christian families enslaved at brick kilns in Pakistan. They work to pay debts, which they can never repay due to accumulated interest. In pictures taken after they are freed, the faces of these families radiate joy. You and I have also been freed from debt; it is release from our burden of sin leading to death. Paul wrote, "And in Him you have been made complete…. When you were dead in your wrongdoings. . . . He made you alive together with Him, having forgiven us all our wrongdoings, having canceled the certificate of debt consisting of decrees against us, which was hostile to us; and He has taken it out of the way, having nailed it to the cross" (Col. 2:10, 13–14 NASB). That is a happy day! "Now may the God of hope fill you with all joy and peace as you believe in Him, so that you may overflow with hope by the power of the Holy Spirit" (Rom. 15:13). We are complete in Christ in whom all the fullness of the Deity, the Father, the Son, and the Holy Spirit dwell in bodily form. In him, we were buried in baptism, and through faith raised from the dead with him (Col. 2:9–12). We do not look from afar on Jesus' death; we are in him, our sins died with him, and we are raised from the dead with him.

Like the families whose freedom has been purchased, our freedom from sin has been bought with a price. "Do you not know that your body is a temple of the Holy Spirit who is in you, whom you have received from God? You are not your own; you were bought at a price" (1 Cor. 6:19–20). "[Jesus] gave Himself for us to redeem us from all lawlessness and to purify for Himself a people for His own possession, zealous for good deeds" (Titus 2:14).

The price of redemption was his life, given for us even when we were dead in our trespasses and sins. C. S. Lewis wrote, "The value of each human soul considered simply in itself, out of relation to God, is zero. . . . The value of the individual does not lie in him. He is capable of receiving value. He receives it by union with Christ."[5] Paul shows how we have gone from zero value to great value: "By nature, we are children of wrath . . . But God, who is rich in mercy, because of His great love with which He loved us, made us alive together with Christ … and raised us up together . . . in the heavenly places in Christ Jesus" (Eph. 2:3–5). Our challenge is to understand we live not in zero, but in heavenly places in Christ Jesus because we are of immense value to him and in him.

The Yoke of Jesus

There are paradoxes in the Bible that we are familiar with: God loved us and saved us in spite of our being sinful children of wrath; God chose and set his love on Israel even when they were the fewest of all people; Jesus became poor so we could be rich; "when I am weak, then I am strong;" we die to self to gain abundant life and to become a royal priesthood. In another unfathomable paradox, Almighty God, Creator of the universe, came as "the Son of Man, not to be served, but to serve, and to give His life as a ransom for many" (Matt. 20:28). A repeated biblical paradox is that we are freed from a yoke of bondage to sin and then become yoked to Jesus. The symbol of the yoke of slavery or oppression is repeatedly used in the Old Testament, often in prophecies of Jesus who will break the yoke.

A beautiful prophecy in Isaiah speaks of Jesus shattering "the yoke of burden."

> The people walking in darkness have seen a great light; on those living in the land of the shadow of death, a light has dawned. You have enlarged the nation and increased its joy. The people rejoice before You as they rejoice at harvest time, as men rejoice in dividing the plunder. For as in the day of Midian You have shattered the yoke of their burden, the bar across their shoulders, and the rod of their oppressor. . . . For unto us a child is born, unto us a son is given, and the government will be upon His shoulders. And He will be called Wonderful Counselor, Mighty God, Everlasting Father, Prince of Peace (Is. 9:2–4, 6).

As we see in this passage, God repeatedly freed the Israelites from the yoke of their enemies, the Midianites, Philistines, Moabites, and Amalekites among others. In addition, this Isaiah 9 prophecy of shattering the yoke is a prophecy of the penalty of sin and death broken in Jesus, who would be born the Mighty God, Everlasting Father, and Prince of Peace.

Jesus often repeated Old Testament themes to show that he fulfilled the Scripture prophecies concerning the Messiah. The breaking of the yoke is one of these themes. The burdensome yoke of sin is traded for the easy yoke of Jesus. Matthew records Jesus in Chapter 11; "Come to me, all you who are weary and burdened, and I will give you rest. Take my yoke upon you and learn from me, for I am gentle and humble in heart, and you will find rest for your souls. For my yoke is easy and my burden is light" (vv. 28–30 NKJV).

In Bible times, matched, experienced oxen yoked together shared equally in their burden; however, to train a young ox to pull a plow, the farmer would yoke it with an older, more experienced animal so that it learned from the older. He did not expect the young ox to share equally, but to learn from the older.[6] When Jesus invited the weary and burdened to take up his yoke, it was an offer to break a heavy yoke of servitude to sin, to replace it with his "easy" yoke and lighter burden by teaching his ways to the one yoked to him. Following in his ways brings rest to their soul. Isaiah 26 gives us a picture of that rest: "You will keep him in perfect peace, whose mind *is* stayed on You, because he trusts in You" (v. 3 NKJV).

Jesus' invitation is sweet and compassionate: "Come to me." Out of love we are created and called to salvation. We can trust him to fulfill obligations towards us; "The One who calls you is faithful" (1Thess. 5:24). He knows the strength of our shoulders and will shape our burdens accordingly.

Instead of coming to Christ, we can be guilty of laying the burden of being good and pleasing God on ourselves; this is not a burden we are meant to carry in our own strength. David wrote in Psalm 38, "For my iniquities have overwhelmed me; they are a burden too heavy to bear" (v. 4). Do you feel burdened with heavy loads on your shoulders? Jesus invites us to come to him and take his yoke where we will find freedom and rest in union with him; it is a choice we make every day in all circumstances. Paul warned, "Stand firm, then, and do not be encumbered once more by a yoke of slavery" (Gal. 5:1). When we take the yoke of Jesus, he is the leader; as the learners, we follow in his ways. His promise is that we will find rest for our souls.

Contemplating His Ways

Paul wrote that as we reflect the glory of the Lord, we are being transformed into his likeness with increasing glory (2 Cor. 3:18). What are some changes you have experienced in your life that have brought you closer to the image of the Lord with increasing glory?

Psalm 22, the Psalm of the Cross, is a great contrast to the next Psalm 23, the Psalm of the Good Shepherd. The incredibly accurate prophecy of Jesus' sufferings on the cross is contrasted with the joy, tranquility, and triumph of Psalm 23. As different as these two descriptions of our Savior are, what threads of likeness do you see in the character and role of Jesus in the two psalms? What does it teach you about Jesus' role in your life?

What are the characteristics of God's chosen people in the 1 Peter 2 passage below? What is your reaction to each one?
> But you are a chosen people, a royal priesthood, a holy nation, a people for God's own possession, to proclaim the virtues of Him who called you out of darkness into His marvelous light. Once you were not a people, but now you are the people of God; once you had not received mercy, but now you have received mercy (1 Peter 2: 9–10).

CHAPTER 17

WALKING THE PATHS OF THE LORD

*All the paths of the Lord are lovingkindness and truth
to those who keep His covenant and His testimonies*
PSALM 25:10, NASB 1995

The bus stopped in the Brazilian darkness, no lights, nothing but black night. "This is your stop," the driver said in Portuguese, but the bus coming to a stop was the real signal Evan understood! He got out and the bus pulled away. He stood in darkness for about 20 minutes until a light appeared. It was his contact from the church where he would preach the next day. This was the kind of adventure that he had whispered about to God as he stepped out our front door on one of his ministry trips. Maybe it was to Brazil, Kenya, Pakistan, Cambodia, or the Philippines, when he said to God, "Well, Lord, we are on an adventure again, aren't we?" The miracles of salvation and healing that he saw as he spoke in churches and places like the Kibera slum in Kenya, bolstered his faith to where he completely trusted God to use him and to keep him safe even in dangerous situations that he faced.

He would need that trust later, on the day he was diagnosed with Lou Gehrig's Disease, also known as ALS. I remember walking down the hall of the hospital after that doctor visit. I realized nothing would ever be the same.

I put one foot in front of the other pushing Evan's wheelchair, isolated as if in a bubble from the bustle of the hospital, confronting the reality of the frailty of life, but at the same time the reality of God's promise of eternal life, his grace, and his peace for that day and the coming days. Evan's and my devotion to our God did not waver. We trusted him with our lives. We chose to walk in his light, yoked to him, and there we learned his faithfulness, and found his yoke easy and his burden light. We were not alone on the journey.

What is it like to walk the paths of the Lord with him? The metaphor of being yoked to Jesus from the previous chapter, is a picture of nearness, or intimacy, as we journey through life. We turn to this theme now.

INTIMACY IN THE YOKE OF JESUS

The idea of union with Jesus implies intimacy in a close, trusting relationship with him. He wants this intimacy to become the utmost treasure in our lives. The Bible is full of glimpses of God's tender love and care for his people that demonstrate this intimacy he desires to have with his children.

The Loving Devotion of God

> *I led them with cords of kindness, with ropes of love; I lifted the yoke from their necks and bent down to feed them.*
> HOSEA 11:4

"Why did Jesus tell us to come here to Galilee? He told us at Passover, the angel at the empty tomb told us, and he told the women at the tomb that we should meet him here. So we came, and look, nothing is happening." Peter could not sit and wait any longer. "I'm going fishing!"

"We're going too!" James and John, Thomas, Nathaniel, and two others immediately jumped into the boat for a night of fishing. Morning came and they hadn't caught anything.

"My little children, don't you have any fish?" a man called from the shore.

"No," they answered.

"If you cast the net on the right side of the boat, you will find some," the man called out.

When they followed his direction, the net filled so full of fish that they could not pull it in to shore. John, the disciple whom Jesus loved, suddenly exclaimed, "It is the Lord!" Indeed, it was Jesus by the fire with fish and bread, which he prepared and gave to them for breakfast (See John 21:1-14).

I love this story. John, who was perhaps the youngest and closest disciple to Jesus, was the first to recognize him on the shore. When he saw the net suddenly full of fish, he knew for sure he was witnessing a miracle and cried out, "It is the Lord!" He was the first to recognize the tone of voice, style, and action of Jesus with whom he had spent so much time and whom he had followed closely and loved deeply. Like John, we have the wonderful opportunity of becoming so familiar with the voice and actions of Jesus from communion with him that we also realize when we are seeing and hearing his truth and experiencing his love and direction. Let's look at two more intimate encounters with Jesus that John shares with us.

Years after seeing the risen Lord on the shore of the Sea of Galilee, John wrote in his gospel how anyone can have an intimate relationship with God. John may have been thinking back to the final Passover when Jesus prayed to the Father words which must have both amazed and comforted all the disciples as they listened; "I in them and You in Me ... so that the world may know that You sent Me and have loved them just as You have loved Me. And I have made Your name known to them and will continue to make it known, so that the love You have for Me may be in them, and I in them" (John 17:23, 26). The answer to Jesus' prayer could not mean anything other than the great love that God has for Jesus will be and is the same great love that God has for us! It could not be more glorious. This love has been poured out on us because Jesus made his Father's name known to us and the Spirit of Jesus himself is in us with all that wondrous, continuous love he has from the Father. Jesus wants us to experience his Father's love the way that he experienced his love. This we do in intimate communion with Jesus. This added communion with God is exactly what Jesus offers us when he comes to abide in us and brings with him the love of the Father. This is the wondrous indwelling when "he who unites himself with the Lord is one with Him in spirit" (1 Cor. 6:17).

The Old Testament offers glimmers of this future intimacy with God through loving relationship with Jesus and his Spirit. Prophetic writings exhibit a perfect balance of awe and reverence before God along with the sympathy, compassion, and nearness of God for his created ones. For example, Isaiah writes, "For thus says the One who is high and lifted up, who inhabits eternity, whose name is Holy: 'I dwell in a high and holy place, and with the oppressed and humble in spirit, to restore the spirit of the lowly and revive the heart of the contrite'" (57:15). In Psalm 33:13–15, we read "The Lord looks from heaven; He sees all the sons of mankind; from His dwelling place He looks out on all the inhabitants of the earth, He who fashions the hearts of them all, He who understands all their works" (NASB). Isaiah, David, and psalm writers demonstrate to us both the greatness of God and his intimate relationship with each individual.

Acts of God from the Old Testament demonstrate his compassion for the oppressed, the lowly, and the contrite. In Exodus, God gives the Ten Commandments to the Israelite people, but he also has detailed statutes for how to treat others. He warns, "If you take your neighbor's cloak as collateral, return it to him by sunset, because his cloak is the only covering he has for his body. What else will he sleep in? And if he cries out to Me, I will hear, for I am compassionate" (22:26–27). What is God's message here? It reminds us not only that God stands for justice in personal relationships, but also that He Himself is intimately involved in the life of each person. In these verses, God shows He is aware of the physical and emotional needs of each of his children, and with great compassion intervenes on their behalf.

The poor neighbor who borrows and gives his cloak as security needs to have it returned before night, so he doesn't get cold without it. The poor laborer should be paid every day since he depends on it to feed his family. The workers harvesting grain, olives, and grapes, should leave some for needy foreigners, orphans, and widows (Deut. 24). Remember how Ruth and Naomi survived by gleaning wheat in Boaz's fields?

The mercy and compassion of God is the same today as when He spoke through Moses. This is why as those who have seen his salvation and live to God, we are obligated to show God's love and care for the poor, the foreigner, the widow, and the fatherless. It was not only the needy who benefited from these laws, but God says to the ones who show his mercy and compassion, "The Lord your God will bless you in all you do" (Deut. 24:19b). God's reason for giving these laws for the poor and oppressed is repeatedly explained in this chapter in Deuteronomy: "Always remember that you were slaves in Egypt and that the LORD your God redeemed you from your slavery" (vv. 18, 22). Each one of us is the object of God's loving care as one who bears His name and carries His glory. God is not too big or too busy to care about whether I have a blanket, or if I get paid on time. In turn, we should remember that God through Jesus has redeemed each of us from slavery to sin in a similar way the Israelites were freed from slavery in Egypt. This is why we must allow God to show his mercy and grace through us to those we come in contact with, regardless of social or economic status. This is how God uses those who are yoked to him; his love and his blessing demonstrate his promise that his yoke is easy, and his burden is light.

Other beautiful passages in the Old Testament show the love relationship God has with his people. When Moses said his good-byes to the children of Israel as they were about to cross over the Jordan River to the Promised Land, he appointed Joshua as leader and taught the people the Song of Moses. It included not only prophecies and warnings of their future rebellion, but also soaring praise to God and reminders of the Lord's love and care for them. He sang that the Lord's portion and inheritance is his people, Jacob, whom he found in "a howling wilderness. He surrounded him, He instructed him, He guarded him as the apple of His eye. As an eagle stirs up its nest and hovers over its young, He spread His wings to catch them and carried them on His pinions" (Deut. 32:10–11). One of my favorite verses is in the next chapter; "The beloved of the Lord shall dwell in safety by Him, who shelters him all the day long; and he shall dwell between His shoulders" (33:12, NKJV). This is where God wants you and me, his beloved ones, to live—between his shoulders, in the safety of constant communion with him. It is where the Apostle John dwelled, both literally and spiritually, between the shoulders of Jesus. The more time we spend there, the more, like John, we come to know the voice of God, understand his ways, and are changed to be like him.

In this day of cell phones and internet, we are used to constant communication either with family and friends, or someone who wants to sell us something. Just think, God had constant communication figured out before time began! Remember the Spirit of God hovering over the waters? Either God, Jesus, or the Holy Spirit has spoken audibly or through scripture, or appeared to people throughout thousands of years. As Deuteronomy 32 above says, God surrounds, instructs, and guards the apple of his eye, you and me! From Job to Paul to you and me, God reaches out to his sons and daughters and delights in their prayers as earthly fathers delight in their children.

Paul wrote, "because you are sons, God sent the Spirit of His Son into our hearts, crying out, 'Abba, Father!'" (Gal. 4:6). Abba, is used even today as the affectionate Hebrew title children use for their father, like we use Daddy. It is by the Spirit of Jesus that we can use this endearing title to our Father. How amazing that the Lord of Hosts, the Almighty God, the Lord our Righteousness allows us to speak to him with such intimacy. Our Abba wants us to be anxious for nothing, but in everything, by prayer and petition, with thanksgiving, present our requests to him. Then his great peace that is beyond our comprehension will guard our hearts and minds in Christ Jesus (Phil. 4:6–7, my paraphrase). Do you hear the lovingkindness of God in this message?

David and Intimacy

No one in the Old Testament expressed a more intimate relationship with God than David. In the book of Psalms, he speaks of living in the presence of God, writing, "How blessed is the one whom You choose and bring near to You to dwell in Your courts. We will be satisfied with the goodness of Your house, Your holy temple" (Ps. 65:4 NASB); and "You have made known to me the path of life; You will fill me with joy in Your presence, with eternal pleasures at Your right hand" (Ps. 16:11);

Psalm 139 is a beautiful expression of God's intimate relationship with each individual. In this psalm David shows that we were in God's presence when he formed us in our mother's womb; he wrote in his book all the days that he planned for each of us. God's thoughts about us number more than the grains of sand so that David wrote, "When I awake, I am still with You" (Ps. 139:18); God's thoughts are constantly on us, even as we sleep. Because his eye is on us, he knows everything about us; when we sit down, when we rise up; our thoughts, our path and when we lie down. God hears and knows every word we speak and our anxieties. David writes, "You have encircled me; you have placed your hand on me. This wondrous knowledge is beyond me. It is lofty; I am unable to reach it" (Ps. 139:5–6 CSB).

Intimacy in the Holy Spirit

> *Now he who keeps His commandments abides in Him,*
> *and He in him. And by this we know that He abides in us,*
> *by the Spirit whom He has given us.*
> 1 JOHN 3:24 NKJV

The greatness, yet nearness of God is incomprehensible and wonderful for us as well as for David who wrote this in Psalm 139 above, but unlike David, we have the revealed mystery of the gospel of Jesus to add to our knowledge of God. David spoke of being in the courts of the Lord. As believers today we also have the right to enter the courts of the Lord with thanksgiving and praise. In addition, we have Jesus' promise spoken to his Father, "We will make our home with them," that foreshadows the indwelling of the Holy Spirit, God in us. In fact, the promised Holy Spirit is proof that God has united us to himself (1 John 3:24). It is how we have the position of holiness before him as saints, or those who are set apart for God's purposes. God calls us to be holy not only in our position as redeemed by faith, but in practical living.

At Pentecost, John, the disciple Jesus loved, witnessed the coming of the Holy Spirit with a miraculous mighty, rushing wind, flames of fire, speech in other languages, and then thousands repenting and believing in Jesus. This is what he wrote about how God makes his abode in us; "By this we know that we abide in Him, and He in us, because He has given us of His Spirit;" and then the requirement for the indwelling Spirit, "Whoever confesses that Jesus is the Son of God, God abides in him, and he in God." The blessing of abiding in God is, "And we have known and believed the love that God has for us. God is love, and he who abides in love abides in God, and God in him" (1 John 4:13, 15–16 NKJV).

Jesus gave the gift of the Holy Spirit when he left the earth in order to continue the intimate relationship he had with his followers and to have that same relationship with all future believers. This is the advantage of the Holy Spirit that we enjoy even today through repentance and belief in Jesus, and which draws us into union with him. Jesus described the role of the Spirit of truth, "There is so much more I want to tell you, but you can't bear it now. When the Spirit of truth comes, he will guide you into all truth. He will not speak on his own but will tell you what he has heard. He will tell you about the future. He will bring me glory by telling you whatever he receives from me" (John 16:12–14 NLT). Our part is to acknowledge the presence of the Holy Spirit and open our ears and our hearts to him, which means we are also open to the Father and the Son.

In one of our final conversations, Evan told me, "There is such freedom in operating in the Spirit. He leads and guides. He is responsible. I am so grateful to God for what He has done, letting me experience that."

It is important to understand that the Holy Spirit is a person, a divine member of the Trinity along with God the Father and Jesus the Son. R. A. Torrey has written an excellent sermon about the person of the Holy Spirit. He says that in order to understand the work of the Holy Spirit, we must understand him as a person, worthy of our entire adoration, love, and worship. Otherwise, we rob a divine being, not giving him the love and surrender to himself that is due. Here is an excerpt from that sermon.

> If we think of the Holy Spirit as so many do as merely a power or influence, our constant thought will be, "How can I get more of the Holy Spirit," but if we think of Him in the Biblical way as a Divine Person, our thought will rather be, "How can the Holy Spirit have more of me?". . . If we once grasp the thought that the Holy Spirit is a Divine Person of infinite majesty, glory and holiness and power, who in marvelous condescension has come into our hearts to make His abode there and take possession of our lives and make use of them, it will put us in the dust and keep us in the dust. I can think of no thought more humbling or more overwhelming than the thought that a person of Divine majesty and glory dwells in my heart and is ready to use even me. . . .
>
> Thousands of men and women can testify to the blessing that has come into their own lives as they have come to know the Holy Spirit, not merely as a gracious influence (emanating, it is true, from God) but as a real Person, just as real as Jesus Christ Himself, an ever-present, loving Friend and mighty Helper, who is not only always by their side but dwells in their heart every day and every hour and who is ready to undertake for them in every

emergency of life. Thousands of ministers, Christian workers and Christians in the humblest spheres of life have spoken to me, or written to me, of the complete transformation of their Christian experience that came to them when they grasped the thought (not merely in a theological, but in an experimental way) that the Holy Spirit was a Person and consequently came to know Him.[7]

This realization of the Holy Spirit as a real person and mighty helper empowered my husband, Evan, in his ministry. As he looked back on his life, he told me, "I learned to listen to him. It's probably the most important lesson in my life. I learned that in my ministry. Everywhere I went I asked him what he wanted me to do, and every time I saw miracles. I've explored those depths as deeply as I could. As I prayed for that girl in Brazil with greatly deformed legs, I went into the deepest place I could with God and asked what I should pray for."

The girl was miraculously healed.

The Holy Spirit has all the characteristics of personality-- knowledge, will, feeling, and emotion. Here are examples from Scripture that demonstrate these qualities of the Holy Spirit.

Knowledge:

> But God has revealed it to us by the Spirit. The Spirit searches all things, even the deep things of God. We have not received the spirit of the world, but the Spirit who is from God, that we may understand what God has freely given us (1 Cor. 2:10, 12).

The Holy Spirit is the Spirit of truth, teaching us the deep things of God.

Will:

> Now when they had gone through Phrygia and the region of Galatia, they were forbidden by the Holy Spirit to preach the word in Asia (Acts 16:6, NKJV).
>
> There are different gifts, but the same Spirit. . . . All these are the work of one and the same Spirit, who apportions them to each one as He determines (1 Cor. 12:4, 11).

The Spirit told Paul not to go to Asia as he had intended. The Holy Spirit uses us and gifts us according to his perfect and loving will, not our own will. This frees us to rely on the Holy Spirit, the divine person; he will direct us.

Personality, Feelings and Emotion:

> Now I urge you, brothers, by our Lord Jesus Christ and by the love of the Spirit, to join me in my struggle by praying to God for me (Rom. 15:30).
>
> The Spirit of the Lord is on Me, because He has anointed Me to preach good news to the poor. He has sent Me to proclaim liberty to the captives and recovery of sight to the blind, to release the oppressed, to proclaim the year of the Lord's favor (Luke 4:18-19).
>
> And do not grieve the Holy Spirit of God, in whom you were sealed for the day of redemption (Eph. 4:30).
>
> Just think how much worse the punishment will be for those who have trampled on the Son of God, and have treated the blood of the covenant, which made us holy, as if it were common and unholy, and have insulted and disdained the Holy Spirit who brings God's mercy to us (Heb. 10:29 NLT).

In summary, the passages above show us that the person of the Holy Spirit loves us. It was he who sent Jesus to preach the gospel, free captives, give sight to the blind, free the oppressed, and reveal it was time for redemption in Jesus. We grieve the Spirit by sinful thoughts or actions. It is the Spirit of grace that we insult, or treat with contempt if we count the blood of Jesus worthless.

Only those who are in union with Jesus by faith in his saving work are capable of receiving the gift of the Holy Spirit. In him we have knowledge and possession of a life of righteousness. In him our spirits are sealed, put in contact with, and molded into the likeness of God, who sanctifies us to make us holy and pleasing to him (Rom. 12:1). The Spirit is our teacher and guide as we walk the paths of the Lord. In the next chapter we will look more closely at how his spiritual gifts enable us to carry out the works of God on earth.

Contemplating His Ways

In Zephaniah 3, the word "midst," or "among" is repeated several times. Read the chapter; why do you think "midst" is repeated? What theme is it tied to?

How do we know that John was likely the closest to Jesus? You can search online, "Who was the disciple that Jesus loved?"

Think about the relationship you have with the Holy Spirit. Does he play the role of comforter, advocate, helper, guide, and teacher of the deep things of God? How can you grieve the Holy Spirit?

CHAPTER 18

DOING THE WORKS OF JESUS

*Truly, truly, I tell you, whoever believes in Me will also
do the works that I am doing.*
JOHN 14:12

Karnak Temple near Luxor, Egypt is a huge 200-acre complex of religious temples, chapels, great halls, pylons, and obelisks. It was built over a period of 2,000 years beginning around 2,000 BC until 30 BC. Each new king made his mark by adding or subtracting as he wished (for some unknown reason, one female pharaoh's images, name, and even an obelisk were defaced or destroyed). Several pairs of huge, monumental walls called pylons stand on each side of the entrance to the Karnak temple complex as well as at different sections within the complex. One of the last pairs of pylons to be built was never finished. They were likely intended to be about 60 feet tall, one section to the right, and one to the left of an entrance within the complex. These pylons formed the entry to a great hall beyond where 134 massive, heavily carved columns were arranged in 16 rows.

The pylons and huge columns are amazing and impressive, but the discovery that intrigued me most was the pile of dried black mud up against the unfinished interior face of the pylon. It wasn't just mud, however. You could see it had been in the form of bricks that had eroded over thousands of years. Piled up against the pylon, the mud bricks formed a ramp for hauling heavy building materials up to the top during construction. When construction stopped, this ramp was never removed. This kind of brick was not only used for construction ramps, but also to build palaces of the kings and common structures as well.

These were the type of mud bricks that the Israelites made under hard labor for building supply cities in the land of Goshen in the Nile delta. Looking at this eroded mud ramp, I pictured God's people forced by cruel taskmasters to make bricks like these day after day. The hope was to wear them down, so they were no longer a threat to the Egyptians. They had thrived in number, wealth, and might so that the king feared they would join enemy armies and leave Egypt. Eventually, to make their labor even more punishing, Pharaoh commanded the taskmasters to stop giving straw that was needed for the bricks and to require the Israelites to gather it themselves without reducing their daily quota.

Pharoah's commands were cruel, meant to break the will and weaken the power of the Israelites. In contrast, God's commandments are for our good, to show his love, righteousness, and justice. Obeying his commands and doing his will shows him our love and faith and is accounted as righteousness. "For this is the love of God, that we keep his commandments. And his commandments are not burdensome, because everyone born of God overcomes the world. And this is the victory that has overcome the world: our faith" (1 John 5:3–4).

God rescued his people from this harsh slavery, leading them to "a good and large land, to a land flowing with milk and honey." He was with them every step of the way on this journey to the Promised Land. "The Lord went before them in a pillar of cloud to guide their way by day, and in a pillar of fire to give them light by night, so that they could travel by day or night" (Ex. 13:21). Their escape from Egypt with Moses at the head is a foreshadowing of God's deliverance from sin and death through Jesus. This deliverance is the gospel story of the New Testament. I hope it is your story!

As ones who are freed from sin, instead of a pillar of cloud or fire, we have the life of Jesus within and the Holy Spirit's presence guiding us on this journey of life. When we abide in Christ, and seek his will, his life and actions are manifested through our faith and actions. "Whoever claims to abide in Him must walk as Jesus walked" (1 John 2:6). Let's take a look together at how we can walk as Jesus walked, or in other words, live his likeness in this world. Jesus said, "Truly, truly, I tell you, whoever believes in Me will also do the works that I am doing" (John 14:12).

DOING THE WILL OF GOD LIKE JESUS

I do not seek My own will, but the will of Him who sent Me.
JOHN 5:30

"Whatever He says to you, do it."
JOHN 2:5 (NKJV)

A first step in doing the works of Jesus is to make the decision like Jesus did, to do the will of God. It is clear that Jesus' main purpose in life was to do the will of his Father. Mary knew this when she told the servants at the wedding to do whatever Jesus said to do, even though he had never publicly done any miracles. She knew he did not seek his own will or his own glory. She had seen his zeal for God, his true Father, and had faith that his instructions would benefit those at the wedding. The prophecy of Jesus in Psalm 40:7-8 shows this truth—"It is written about me in the scroll: I delight to do Your will, O my God." Ultimately, God's will was for Jesus to provide salvation for all people, a plan that was formed in the mind of God before time began. As his sacrificial death drew near, Jesus fervently prayed to be delivered from death on the cross. But just as in his lifelong obedience to God, in that final hour in the Garden of Gethsemane, he prayed, "Yet not as I will, but as You will" (Matt. 26:39).

God's plan for Jesus was written "in the scroll." In a similar way, David speaks of himself and says, "all my days were written in Your book and ordained for me before one of them came to be" (Ps. 139:16). We have the same calling to do the will of God that was planned for us and written in God's book. "He has saved us and called us to a holy calling . . . by His own purpose and by the grace He granted us in Christ Jesus before time began" (2 Tim. 1:9). God's purpose for us begins with obeying his will.

In closing his letter to the church in Thessalonica, Paul writes a very clear summary of how to obey God's will in their position "in Christ Jesus," in other words, those who have entered into union with him by faith. He urged them, "*Always* be joyful. *Never* stop praying. Be thankful in *all* circumstances, for this is God's will for you who belong to Christ Jesus. Do not stifle the Holy Spirit. Do not scoff at prophecies, but test *everything* that is said. Hold on to what is good. Stay away from *every* kind of evil" (1 Thess. 5:16–22 NLT, emphasis mine). Pay attention to what the absolute words always, never, all, everything, and every signal. Acknowledging the Holy Spirit's leading in all circumstances is absolute, complete obedience to the way of Jesus. Whatever he says to you, do it. How do we know what Jesus is saying to us today? It comes from reading and meditating on his word, which acquaints us with his ways, and with his Spirit that lives in us.

Jesus delighted only and always in the Father's will; "I can do nothing by Myself; I judge only as I hear. And My judgment is just, because I do not seek My own will, but the will of Him who sent Me" (John 5:30). Like Jesus who came in human flesh, we can do nothing by ourselves, but need to seek God's will, not our own. Can we say, "I can do nothing by myself; I judge only as I hear. I do not seek my own will, but God's will so that my judgment is just?" God's ways are so much higher than ours, it's likely that many of our plans have come from our own thoughts and habits, not his. This means it's necessary to align our actions and thinking with his and not operate solely on our own. We strive to think his thoughts, do what he does, and love whom he loves. Again, that comes from time spent with him is his Word and listening to his Spirit.

Psalm One describes the one who delights, or takes pleasure in, the Lord; "He is like a tree planted by streams of water that yields its fruit in its season, and its leaf does not wither. In all that he does, he prospers.... for the Lord knows the way of the righteous, but the way of the wicked will perish" (vv. 3, 6 ESV). Absolute words are used for absolute truth; the righteous man who delights in the Lord prospers in *all* he does, but the wicked will perish. Prospering in all things is a promise for the one seeking the righteousness of God. It does not mean they won't make mistakes in their efforts to do the will of God, but that in contrast to the wicked, because they have the righteousness of God, a righteousness that is by faith, "he will sustain you to the end, so that you will be blameless on the day of our Lord Jesus Christ. God, who has called you into fellowship with His Son Jesus Christ our Lord, is faithful" (1 Cor. 1:8–9).

EXERCISING THE POWER OF JESUS

I also labor, striving according to His power
which works mightily within me.
COLOSSIANS 1:29, NASB

The Sea of Galilee is really a freshwater lake, a little more than twelve miles long and seven miles wide. Because it is about 680 feet below sea level, the water can get quite warm. In fact, this is why tropical fruits such as bananas and mangoes grow near its shores. When cold air flows down from the surrounding hills and collides with the warm air off the lake, sudden violent storms come up. My travel group in Israel was scheduled to take a boat ride on the lake but the operator said there was danger of a storm that day, so it was canceled. There was no indication of a storm in the forecast, and the lake appeared calm all day while we were in the area. We had to laugh about the furious storm that was coming at any moment and had fun coming up with scenarios that could have caused the cancellation. It really was a thrill just to wade in the water, and have my devotions one morning sitting beside the Sea of Galilee.

Matthew, Mark, and John all tell the story of the disciples caught up in one of the storms on the lake. Mark's version of the story states that earlier in the day, John the Baptist's disciples had come to Jesus to tell him that Herod had beheaded John the Baptist. When Jesus heard it, he went by boat to a deserted place, but crowds from surrounding cities ran to him. Jesus had compassion on them, like sheep without a shepherd, and began to teach them many things. Late in the afternoon, Jesus knew the crowd needed something to eat. He miraculously multiplied five loaves and two fish and with the disciples serving, fed five thousand people. He immediately sent his disciples across to the other side of the lake in the boat. This is when Jesus finally found time to go to the mountain to pray.

Then, during the fourth watch of the night, Jesus saw the disciples struggling to row against the high wind. He went to them, walking on the sea. The disciples cried out in fear, thinking he was a ghost, but Jesus called to them, "Don't be afraid, it is I." He got into the boat, and the wind stopped. The disciples were utterly astounded, and marveled. They knew Psalm 107 that described the power of God, and God alone, that "caused the storm to be still, so that the waves of the sea were hushed" (v. 29). Now they had just seen Jesus do a miracle that they knew only God could do. It was the power of Jesus to calm the sea that amazed the disciples and brought them closer to believing he truly was the Son of God (Mark 6).

Jesus' followers discovered in many circumstances that God "is able to do immeasurably more than all we ask or imagine, according to His power that is at work within us" (Eph.3:20). In the same way, God's power is available to us today in more ways than we can imagine. In his book, *Engines of Heaven,* Evan wrote about miracles that he saw in his ministry in other countries. He told me that at first, he was surprised when people were healed, but that changed to surprise when they weren't. Sometimes God would show him why not and then that person would be healed at the next service. He looked at his hands in wonder that God would use him to heal and bring God's love to many souls. Not only that, but he knew God was protecting him. The most dangerous place he went to was Pakistan. There was always a man with an AK-47 on the stage with him when he spoke. One time, the service was cut short when a report came in that "some bad guys" were coming in a car with guns, and they needed to break up. Evan touched people who were lined up as he headed out of the area. He heard later that many of those people reported healing in their bodies.

The Ephesians 3:20 verse above is at the end of one of Paul's many powerful prayers that he included in his letters to the churches. Earlier in the prayer he prays, "to the Father from whom every family in heaven and on earth derives its name. I ask that out of the riches of His glory He may strengthen you with power through His Spirit in your inner being." It is the power of the Spirit of Christ that enables us to walk as Jesus walked. Paul prays for the Ephesians to have the strength and power that comes out of the riches of God's glory. How wonderful to know that we have the richness of God's power in our inner being through his Spirit!

We have this treasure, as Paul says, "in jars of clay to show that this surpassingly great power is from God and not from us" (2 Cor. 4:7). When we receive the Holy Spirit, we receive his power and his fruit. It is only by the power of the Holy Spirit and not by our own that his fruit is revealed through our lives. This fruit is his love, his joy, his peace, his patience, his kindness, his goodness, his faithfulness [faith KJV], his gentleness, and his self-control (Gal. 5:22–23). Remember, Jesus is the vine, and we are the branches. The Father is the vinedresser who takes away every branch that does not bear this fruit, and prunes the branches that bear fruit so that they have power to bear even more fruit. The question is, are we as branches connected to the vine of Jesus and allowing his fruit to develop in us? Or, as God spoke of his vineyard, "What more could have been done for My vineyard than I have done for it? Why, when I expected sweet grapes, did it bring forth sour fruit?" (Is. 5:4).

We all have felt the pain of pruning; it is important to remember that God uses difficult times to produce more of his love, joy, patience, kindness, and all other fruit of his Spirit. He wants us to allow his power to work mightily in us. A beautiful illustration of this is the journey of pilgrims through the Valley of Baca, or Weeping, in Psalm 84.

> Blessed are those whose strength is in You,
> whose hearts are set on pilgrimage.
> As they pass through the Valley of Baca,
> they make it a place of springs;
> even the autumn rain covers it with pools.
> They go from strength to strength,
> until each appears before God in Zion (5–7).

This may have been an actual valley that was a difficult, dry place with no water for those going up to Jerusalem to observe a feast. For us it can be a symbol of the journey of life for those intent on walking in God's paths. This is where sorrow and sadness turn into joy, comfort, pleasantness and provision. Only the power of God can make this transformation of dry, barren times into abundant blessings, remembered with gratitude. The power of God can produce abundant fruit in our lives even in the valleys. When we see God working in the face of hardship, we go from strength to even more strength for the coming challenges. As members of the body of Christ and his Spirit within, we have his glorious power to do works worthy of Jesus in all goodness, righteousness, and truth.

GLORIFYING GOD LIKE JESUS

Whether, then, you eat or drink or whatever you do,
do all to the glory of God"
I CORINTHIANS 10:31 NASB

Doing the acts of Jesus means we do the will of God like Jesus did and exercise the power of Jesus. Another imperative the word of God gives us is to glorify God in everything we do. Paul wrote, "Whether, then, you eat or drink or whatever you do, do all to the glory of God." Through the life of the Holy Spirit within, we have the possibility of making every act of our lives give glory to God, giving him honor and praise in every area of life. It is the test to apply to every thought, word and action. Does it advance the glory, honor, and praise of God?

Jonathan Edwards wrote in his "Dissertation Concerning the End for Which God Created the World," that all the Scriptures speak of as God's ultimate goal of his works on earth is in the one phrase, *the glory of God*. To paraphrase Edwards, when people know, esteem, love, rejoice in, and praise God, the glory of God is both seen and acknowledged in them; they receive his fullness and return it. The beams of glory come from God and are reflected back again to him. So, the whole is *of* God and *in* God, and *to* God, and God is the beginning, middle and end of this affair. Jonathan Edwards knew what Jesus said in his Passover prayer to God, "The glory which You have given Me I also have given to them, so that they may be one, just as We are one" (John 17:22 NASB).

Old Testament prophets reveled in the glory of God and showed how to glorify God as the beginning, middle, and end of every aspect of their lives. To them he was the divine and compassionate creator, deliverer, ruler, judge, and source of future salvation. Throughout the Old Testament, prophets give us examples of praising and honoring God which included doing God's will in dangerous and difficult acts of obedience. They wrote about the greatness of God who extends loving devotion to a thousand generations to those who believe and obey his commands. In Exodus the Lord himself passed in front of Moses proclaiming his name and nature, "The Lord, the Lord God, is compassionate and gracious, slow to anger, abounding in loving devotion and faithfulness, maintaining loving devotion to a thousand generations, forgiving iniquity, transgression, and sin" (34:6-7). In loving devotion God offered to mankind forgiveness of sin first through obedience to the law of Moses, and in a much more eternal and glorious way through the perfect sacrifice of his only Son. The writer of Hebrews expresses this beautifully.

> On many past occasions and in many different ways, God spoke to our fathers through the prophets. But in these last days He has spoken to us by His Son, whom He appointed heir of all things, and through whom He made the universe. The Son is the radiance of God's glory and the exact representation of His nature, upholding all things by His powerful word. After He had provided purification for sins, He sat down at the right hand of the Majesty on high (Heb. 1:1–3).

The New Testament is full of stories of those who heard and followed Jesus, and who understood he was the Holy One of God. Their belief in Jesus and how they declared his praise gives us examples for honoring and glorifying the Son of God. One of the most authentic and enthusiastic witnesses for Jesus in the Bible was the woman at the well. The setting for this John 4 story was Jacob's well near Shechem, modern-day Nablus, in Samaria. Jacob purchased the land there when he returned to the area with Leah and Rachel and his children. It would have been normal for Jesus to skirt around Samaria when traveling from Jerusalem to Galilee, either on the flat land near the Jordan River, or farther west to avoid hilly, difficult traveling. It is interesting that even today that area, which is in Arab territory, has no major north-south routes. But another major reason to avoid it in Jesus' day was the great hostility between Jews and the Samaritans who were Jews left behind when the Assyrians conquered the northern kingdom of Israel. These Jews had mixed with other people imported by the Assyrians, or with nearby peoples. That is why when Jesus, weary from the challenging journey, asked the Samaritan woman for a drink, she asked him why he was asking her! He answered her, "If you only knew the gift God has for you and who you are speaking to, you would ask me, and I would give you living water.... But those who drink the water I give will never be thirsty again. It becomes a fresh, bubbling spring within them, giving them eternal life" (John 4:10, 14 NLT).

The woman asked for the water that would make it so she would never get thirsty or have to draw water again. This opened the way for Jesus to point her to true worship of God, and he asked her to go get her husband. When he said he knew she had had five husbands and the one she was with now was not her husband, she concluded he was a prophet. She began to bring up differences of beliefs between Jews and Samaritans about where to worship. Jesus said to her the former way of worship, whether in Jerusalem or on the mountains of Samaria was changing. "Salvation and true worship of God is of the Jews. The Father is seeking those who worship in spirit and truth, because God is Spirit" (vv. 22–24 my paraphrase).

"I know the Messiah is coming—the one who is called Christ. When he comes, he will explain everything to us."

"Jesus answered her, 'I Am the Messiah!'"

The woman immediately left her waterpot and went into the city, calling the men to come see this man who told her all about herself. "Could he possibly be the Messiah?" she said to them. Wanting to see this for themselves, they came to Jesus and heard his words. "Now we believe ... because we have heard him ourselves. Now we know that he is indeed the Savior of the world" (vv. 25–26, 42 NLT).

The Samaritan woman and the men at the village by Jacob's well, honored and glorified Jesus as Savior because of his witness to the woman. As followers of Christ Jesus, we have the same powerful Holy Spirit at work in us as he had, and the same calling to shine the light of the gospel to honor God. The world should see the glory of God illustrated by our lives. Matthew said it this way:

> You are the light of the world. A city set on a hill cannot be hidden; nor do people light a lamp and put it under a

basket, but on the lampstand, and it gives light to all who are in the house. Your light must shine before people in such a way that they may see your good works, and glorify your Father who is in heaven (5:14–16 NASB).

Jesus has entrusted his reputation and his honor to us. Those who might never have seen the revelation of him in the Word of God, could be won to behold him and love him if we Christ-followers clearly show his image in our character and speech. "If anyone speaks, let it be as one who speaks God's words; if anyone serves, let it be from the strength God provides, so that God may be glorified through Jesus Christ in everything" (1 Peter 4:11).

Contemplating His Ways

Look up Barna's seven cornerstones of a biblical worldview. Are you one of the 6% of American adults who actually have a biblical worldview?

Remember WWJD, What Would Jesus Do? Because we are in Christ Jesus and his Spirit is in us, we are equipped with the fruit of the Spirit. What fruit is most important right now to help you walk as Jesus walked?

How has God's power worked through you in words and actions that demonstrated the goodness, righteousness, and truth of Jesus?

CHAPTER 19

LIVING THE ETERNAL LIFE OF JESUS

Our Savior, Christ Jesus, has abolished death and illuminated the way to life and immortality through the gospel.
2 TIMOTHY 1:10

My battle with cancer included three weeks at an alternative cancer clinic in Bavaria, southern Germany. This was a beautiful setting for treatment, with the Alps rising sharply from the plain that ran south from Munich, the nearest major city. The clinic was within walking distance of a cog railway that ascended 3,993 feet to near the top of Mount Wendelstein. The train passed through alpine meadows, forest, and over jagged cliffs. At the top you could see the beautiful white sea of the Alps stretching into Austria. I made friends with women from all over the world during my stay, and the night before leaving for home I invited them to my room for a prayer time. All of us were facing the possibility of losing our lives to cancer. I read some Bible passages about the hope of heaven. In our discussion several of the Christian women and I expressed that we were not afraid to die because we knew we would be instantly with Jesus. Our Ukrainian friend's eyes got big, shock on her face. "You are not afraid to die?" She was amazed that we knew what would happen if we lost our lives to cancer. God opened the door for us to share the gospel with her and give her a Bible. We planted a seed and trusted God for the harvest.

The promise of eternal life is a key message of the Bible. Our understanding of heaven is made clearer by understanding the union of the believer with God in this world. Living in union with Christ on earth helps us understand and prepare for our complete and eternal union with him in heaven. The eternal life of Jesus and his eternal Holy Spirit within us as followers and members of his church will continue after death because we share in the resurrection life of Jesus. Murray wrote, "Why can [the believer] have patience in the perplexities and the adversities of the present? Why can he have confident assurance with reference to the future and rejoice in the hope of the glory of God? It is because he cannot think of past, present, or future apart from union with Christ."[8]

We were chosen before the foundation of the world to be joined to Jesus Christ. We enjoy the sweet presence of the Holy Spirit day by day, and through this union we will be the chosen to share in the glory of heaven. The whole reality of time and eternity is changed when we choose to be united to Jesus through repentance and belief that his death covers our sins. Our union will continue after death whereby we rejoice with joy unspeakable and full of glory.

Evan felt this joy when he faced his final days. Echoing what he said to Jesus heading out the door for an evangelistic trip over the ocean, he now said, "Well Lord, we are on an adventure again, aren't we?" He told me, "I'm on an adventure with him again, how cool. He's my sweet companion all my life. I was a caller of the lost. That's what I am, a caller of the lost. It was God's ministry. He was in charge, not me. I got to see so many people touched by God. It was precious. Now I know what lay up treasures in heaven means. I will see those people there."

I am reminded of the advice Evan told me that he gave a young friend who was preparing her last message as teacher to children's church. "I told her to teach what you would to dying men. She did and five children came to know the Lord. I just cried over that."

The New Testament tells us the most about the grace of God's redemption for dying men and the promise of eternal life in heaven. It contains the story of the new covenant of salvation by grace that Jesus' death and resurrection ushers in to replace the old covenant of works and the system of sacrifices for sin. That said, Jesus declared that he did not come to abolish the Law or the writings of the prophets, but to fulfill them (Matt. 5:17). This tells us that there are old covenant prophecies that Jesus came to fulfill as well as laws for which he demonstrated God's intent and which he expanded to include the element of grace in the salvation he freely gives to undeserving man. In fact, a study of the Hebrew Bible, the Old Testament, can shed great light on New Testament truth.

The resurrection of the dead is not only important in New Testament times, but also in the Old Testament. It is an important part of the story of Abraham and Isaac who lived under covenant promises of God. Abraham is honored for his faith in both the Old Testament and the New. First, Genesis 12:2-3 records the covenant God made with Abraham. "I will make you into a great nation, and I will bless you; I will make your name great, so that you will be a blessing . . . and all the families of the earth will be blessed through you." Repeatedly, God spoke these promises to Abraham and his seed in visions and even appeared as a man, promising that Sarah would have a son and that his descendants would be like the number of stars in the heavens. Genesis 15:6 tells us Abraham believed the Lord and he accounted it to him for righteousness. How hard it must have been for him to take Isaac, his promised son up on Mount Moriah to offer him as a sacrifice as God commanded. After all, it was through Isaac that all the families of the earth were to be blessed.

We learn "the rest of the story" in the New Testament book of Hebrews. It is interesting when New Testament writers elaborate on Old Testament stories like Abraham's. This is how we gain greater insight into the story of Abraham and Isaac. We learn that faith-filled, righteous Abraham was ready to offer up his son, but the book of Hebrews reveals that "Abraham reasoned that God could raise the dead, and in a sense, he did receive Isaac back from death" (11:19).

Abraham did not believe death was the end. He had faith that if he killed Isaac, he would come back from the dead. He knew God had power over life and death and he had complete faith in God's promise that a great nation would come through his son, Isaac. That faith was not misplaced. Israel is today a great nation of God's people, the Jews. They have been a blessing to the world, in particular through Jesus our Savior, born in Abraham's line. In Matthew 8, Jesus told the Roman centurion whose son he healed that "many will come from east and west and recline at table with Abraham, Isaac, and Jacob in the kingdom of heaven." Not only would these patriarchs be at the table in heaven, but also those from other nations, meaning Gentiles, who would share in salvation and everlasting life. Moreover, Jesus' return will be to Jerusalem, the Mount of Olives (Zech. 14:4, Joel 3:16-17). What great blessings and promises come to us through Jesus!

EAGERLY WAITING JESUS' APPEARING

Christ was offered once to bear the sins of many;
and He will appear a second time, not to bear sin,
but to bring salvation to those who eagerly await Him.
HEBREWS 9:28

Job is described as a blameless and upright man, one who feared God and shunned evil (Job 1:1). We are shown the scene in heaven where Satan accuses Job of worshiping God because he had blessed him with great possessions, but if he lost all he had, he would turn away from God and curse him to his face. God agrees to put Job to the test and gives Satan permission to take away his great possessions and also his sons and daughters. Even then, Job honors God, "The Lord gave, and the Lord has taken away. Blessed be the name of the Lord" (Job 1:21). His friends come to mourn and comfort him when they hear of the great tragedy that struck him. They each speak to him but instead of comforting him, they suggest he has displeased God and needs to confess.

Job is steadfast and answers, "I know that my Redeemer lives, and in the end, He will stand upon the earth. Even after my skin has been destroyed, yet in my flesh I will see God. I will see Him for myself; my eyes will behold Him, and not as a stranger. How my heart yearns within me!" (Job 19:25-27). Job has a concept of God, but when God speaks directly to him, he repents of his former speech, realizing his concept of God fell immensely short of his true greatness. In the end, he confesses, "My ears had heard of You, but now my eyes have seen You. Therefore I despise myself, and I repent in dust and ashes" (42:5-6).

Job had always feared God and had faith in him as his Redeemer whom he would see with his own eyes even after death. His horrendous suffering increased his yearning to see God. This same yearning to see God is woven into the New Testament with the added revelation that it would be Jesus, God's Son, who would appear "a second time, not to bear sin, but to bring salvation to those who eagerly await Him" (Heb. 9:28). So, we ask ourselves the question, does my heart yearn to see God? Am I eagerly waiting for his second appearing?

Remember that Paul said, "For you died, and your life is now hidden with Christ in God. When Christ, who is your life, appears, then you also will appear with Him in glory" (Col. 3:3-4). Job knew he would see God and his heart yearned for that time. We also will see God. At Christ's appearing, we will appear with him in the glory of heaven because his life is our life. This is astonishing reality and something to eagerly wait for!

EAGERLY AWAITING THE ONE WHO LOVES US

The LORD your God is among you; He is mighty to save.
He will rejoice over you with gladness; He will quiet you with
His love; He will rejoice over you with singing."
ZEPHANIAH 3:17

> *Jesus Christ, the faithful witness, the firstborn from the dead*
> *and the ruler of the kings of the earth. To him who loves us*
> *and has set us free from our sins by his blood.*
> REVELATION 1:5 (CSB)

In this book, and particularly in Part Two, we have focused on how we are united with Jesus in his death, burial, and resurrection when we trust him as Lord and Savior. Because Jesus conquered sin and death, we also have conquered sin and death. Because he is alive to God, we also are alive to God in Christ Jesus (Rom. 6:9–11).

This is a glorious union which is based on the love of God and of his Son "who loves us and has set us free from our sins by his blood," as the above verse in Revelation 1 says. Let us go back to the cross, which was Jesus' ultimate demonstration of God's love for man and what enables us to forever be in the presence of God.

It is astounding how much Psalm 22 reveals about Jesus' final moments on the cross. This includes even his thoughts and prayers to God, as we will see. Known as the Psalm of the Cross, Psalm 22 unfolds a moving prophecy of how Jesus would lay down his life for us, and in so doing show us what love is (1 John 3:16). We know this psalm is about Jesus from the New Testament Hebrews 2:10–12 passage that indicates the quotes there from Psalm 22 are from Jesus.

There are amazing parallels between this Psalm and the accounts of Jesus' crucifixion in Matthew, Mark, Luke, and John. However, what is unique to Psalm 22 is that it is written in first person, from the perspective of Jesus so we know his thoughts on the cross. Here are a few of the parallels with New Testament references.

Psalm 22:1 My God, my God, why have You forsaken me? (Mark 15:34)

Psalm 22:7 All who see me mock me; they sneer and shake their heads. (Matt. 27:39)

Psalm 22:8 He trusts in the Lord, let the Lord deliver him. (Matt. 27:42)

Psalm 22:16 They have pierced my hands and feet. (Luke 24:39)

Psalm 22:18 They divide my garments among them and cast lots for my clothing. (Matt. 27:35)

Hebrew scholars point out that even today, chapter and verse numbers are not used to identify a Hebrew Bible passage, but rather, the first line of the chapter is quoted. When Jesus said, "My God, My God, why have Your forsaken Me?" the religious Jews at the cross would have been impacted, knowing these were the first words of Psalm 22 and that Jesus was calling attention to this psalm as a prophecy concerning him.

The second part of this psalm is praise to God. It reveals Jesus' prayers to God concerning the future as he nears death. He promises to declare his name and to praise him. At this most difficult moment, his thoughts turn to his brethren. He says, "I will declare Your name to My brethren; In the midst of the assembly I will praise You" (22:22 NKJV). My brethren is a phrase not often used so it is especially important to note its use here and again in John 20:17 where we see that Jesus fulfills this promise to God by asking Mary to announce his resurrection and coming ascension to the disciples. He also assembled with these disciples several times as well as with 500 others before he ascended into heaven.

Jesus' prophetic prayer continues. All the descendants of Jacob will glorify and fear God because he did not turn his back on him on the cross, but heard him in his affliction (22:24). All the ends of the earth, all the families of the nations, and all the prosperous of the earth, will seek and praise God; will turn to the Lord and worship him; and will bow down to him. We have seen this prophecy partially fulfilled in the years since Jesus' death and resurrection and look forward to the time of complete fulfillment.

Finally, he says, the next generation "shall come and proclaim his righteousness to a people yet unborn, that he has done it" (v. 31 ESV). Jesus' prophecy from the cross ends, "He has done it," and John's gospel echoes Jesus' final words, "It is finished" (19:30). Jesus' work of love and saving grace is accomplished. He fulfilled what he said, "And I, if I am lifted up from the earth, will draw all people to Myself" (John 12:32 NASB). God has buried our sin with Christ who has drawn us to himself and made us alive with him. Hallelujah! Let us do our part to glorify him and proclaim his righteousness to all the ends of the earth and all the families of the nations.

EAGERLY WAITING FOR HEAVEN

Evan felt the draw of heaven in his last days. He told me, "I'm not afraid of death. It is victory, not defeat. We have died to sin and are hidden in Christ in heavenly places already, so death is a little blip, a small step. I have felt the splash of that heavenly fountain. The Holy Spirit calls heaven home. Isn't that precious? This body is just a tent. It will release me for the rest God has for me for eternity. We are heavenly beings going into inevitable light." The promise is found in 1 Thessalonians 4:14, "For since we believe that Jesus died and rose again, we also believe that God will bring with Jesus those who have fallen asleep in Him." Our union with him will never be broken.

We are united in a love relationship with Christ Jesus that will continue in heaven. Charles Spurgeon, known as the Prince of Preachers, loved to preach about the cross of Christ; John 12:32 above was one of his favorite verses. He spoke of being "joined to Christ by bands of everlasting love." Long before the worlds were made, Jesus viewed with delight those who would choose to follow him. Spurgeon wrote, "Strong were the indissoluble bands of love which then united Jesus to the souls whom he determined to redeem. . . . Love has a most potent power in effecting and sustaining union, but never does it display its force so well as when we see it bringing the Maker into oneness with the creature, the divine into alliance with the human. This, then, is to be regarded as the dayspring of union, the love of Christ Jesus the Lord."[9]

There is no greater love than Jesus laying down his life for us. Just hours before his death, Jesus comforted his disciples by telling them he was going away to prepare a place for them and would come again to take them to himself "so that where I am you may be also" (John 14:3). What a wondrous thought that Jesus suffered the agonizing death of the cross because ultimately, he wants us, his beloved, to be with him in heaven.

We are assured of our final resurrection, which will be the crowning event of our existence. Moreover, we have this promise "What we will be has not yet appeared; but we know that when he appears we shall be like him, because we shall see him as he is. And everyone who thus hopes in him purifies himself as he is pure." (1 John 3:2–3 ESV).

I hope you have seen in these pages that God wants to be eternally united with you in close communion. Here on earth, "his divine power has granted to us all things that pertain to life and godliness, through the knowledge of him who called us to his own glory and excellence" (2 Peter 1:3 ESV). We have precious and very great promises for living in glory and excellence in the house of the Lord all the days of our lives.

"Though you have not seen Him, you love Him; and though you do not see Him now, you believe in Him and rejoice with an inexpressible and glorious joy" (1 Peter 1:8).

Contemplating His Ways

How does Zephaniah 3:17 affect how you think about yourself?

> The LORD your God is among you; He is mighty to save. He will rejoice over you with gladness; He will quiet you with His love; He will rejoice over you with singing.

Are you eagerly waiting to be with Jesus? Why or why not?

When we realize we have the life of Jesus in us, we understand we live dependent on him. What do you think about this quote from a recent sermon? "Stay dependent on the Father with a heart that has no will of its own."

Use this link to read about all the people that were raised to life in the Bible. These are short, illustrated stories written in simple style that could be used with children. https://www.learnreligions.com/people-raised-from-the-dead-in-the-bible-4109363

NOTES

PART ONE NOTES

1 All Top Everything, "The Top Ten Best Selling Books of All Time," March 5, 2025, https://www.alltopeverything.com/top-10-best-selling-books-of-all-time/

2 Grant Luton, *In His Own Words: Messianic Insights into the Hebrew Alphabet* (Uniontown: Beth Tikkun, 2018), 127.

3 Christopher Eames, "New Research Reveals Dead Sea Scrolls Older Than Previously Thought," June 6, 2025, https://armstronginstitute.org/1235-new-research-reveals-dead-sea-scrolls-older-than-previously-thought.

4 "Dead Sea Scrolls Bible Translations: Frequently Asked Questions," http://dssenglishbible.com/Scrollsfaqs.htm.

5 Jeff A. Benner, "The Great Isaiah Scroll and the Masoretic Text," https://www.ancient-hebrew.org/dss/great-isaiah-scroll-and-the-masoretic-text.htm.

6 "Bryant G. Wood PhD, "The Tel Dan Stela and the Kings of Aram and Israel," https://biblearchaeology.org/research/topics/amazing-discoveries-in-biblical-archaeology/2233-the-tel-dan-stela-and-the-kings-of-aram-and-israel.

7 Ralph Buntyn, "Miracle in the Desert," https://unitedisraelworldunion.com/miracle-in-the-desert/.

8 Hugh Ross, "Fulfilled Prophecy: Evidence for the Reliability of the Bible," https://reasons.org/explore/publications/articles/fulfilled-prophecy-evidence-for-the-reliability-of-the-bible.

9 Alfred Edersheim, *The Life and Times of Jesus the Messiah* (USA: Hendrickson Publishers Marketing, LLC, 1993), 168–173.

10 Alexander MacLaren, *Expositions Of Holy Scripture*. "Matthew: The Tables Turned: The Questioners Questioned." https://biblehub.com/commentaries/matthew/22-34.htm.

11 Luton, p. 230–231.

12 Patsy Stevens, "George Muller," https://gardenofpraise.com/ibdmuller.htm.

13 Admin, "How to Fall in Love with Bible Study According to George Muller," January 18, 2020, https://smartandrelentless.com/how-to-fall-in-love-with-bible-study-according-to-george-muller/.

14 Kristi McLelland, *Rediscovering Israel: A Fresh Look at God's Story in Its Historical and Cultural Context* (Eugene, OR: Harvest House Publishers, 2023), 41–47.

15 For excellent Bible teaching on Jesus in the Old Testament with Jewish culture and Hebrew language insights, see One for Israel, https://www.oneforisrael.org/podcast/.

16 https://biblehub.com/psb/psalms/119.htm.

17 Luton, p. 57–70. Note: *Daleth*, the fourth letter, is also the number four, associated in the Bible with testimony and witness; for example the four gospels present Jesus as King, Servant, Man, and Divine consecutively, further tying this fourth stanza to Jesus.

18 David Reagan, "Desolation and Reclamation of the Land of Israel: Eyewitness Reports," https://www.raptureforums.com/bible-prophecy/desolation-reclamation-land-israel-eyewitness-reports/.

NOTES

19 Tuly Weisz, "Mark Twain's unwittingly prophetic vision for the State of Israel," https://www.jpost.com/Opinion/Unto-the-nations-505760.

20 S. B. Shaw, *The Great Revival in Wales*, (Pensacola: Christian Life Books, 2002), p. 22.

PART TWO NOTES

1 Arthur W. Pink, *Spiritual Union and Communion*, (Lafayette IN: Sovereign Grace Publishers, Inc.,) p. 18.

2 John Murray, *Redemption Accomplished and Applied*, (Grand Rapids: William B. Eerdmans, 1955), 172.

3 John Piper, "Why I Love the Apostle Paul," https://www.desiringgod.org/articles/why-i-love-the-apostle-paul.

4 James Montgomery Boice, *Foundations of the Christian Faith*, (Downers Grove: InterVarsity Press, 1986).

5 Dean Braxton, *What It Feels Like to Die*, (Columbia, SC, Bowler Identified Services, 2019), 15-16. Note: Dean's story is on The 700 Club, https://www.youtube.com/watch?v=c3Zjt8r-hNA.

6 MacLaren, "Philippians: Saving Knowledge," https://biblehub.com/commentaries/philippians/3-10.htm.

7 C. S. Lewis, *Miracles: A Preliminary Study*, (New York: MacMillan, 1947).

8 R. T. Kendall, *The Lord's Prayer*, (Grand Rapids: Chosen Books, 2010), 197.

9. MacLaren, "Isaiah: The Sucker from the Felled Oak," https://biblehub.com/commentaries/ isaiah/11-1.htm.

PART THREE NOTES

1 John McKeel, "Peter's Wife, Sarah's Daughter," https://johnmckeel.com/bible-study/peters-wife-sarahs-daughter/.

2. MacLaren, "Partakers of the Divine Nature," https://biblehub.com/commentaries/2_peter/1-4.htm.

3. Evan Wiggs, *Engines of Heaven*, (Xlibris Corporation, 2013), p. 234.

4. Barnes' Notes on the Bible, https://biblehub.com/commentaries/hebrews/3-14.htm.

5. C. S. Lewis, *The Weight of Glory*, (New York: HarperOne Publishers, 1976, revised 1980), p. 170, 174.

6. Luton, p. 118.

7. R. A. Torrey, "The Person and Work of The Holy Spirit," https://biblehub.com/library/torrey/the_person_and_work_of_the_holy_spirit/chapter_i_the_personality_of.htm.

8. Murray, p. 174.

9. Charles Spurgeon, "Bands of Love: Or, Union to Christ," https://archive.spurgeon.org/s_and_t/bol1865.php.

www.ingramcontent.com/pod-product-compliance
Lightning Source LLC
LaVergne TN
LVHW051116080426
835510LV00018B/2079